MW01092617

# Strategy and Grand Strategy

Joshua Rovner

'In this instructive, historically-informed analysis, Joshua Rovner probes the sometimes surprising relationship between 'grand strategy' – a state's political-military theory of security – and 'strategy' – effectively a state's military theory about how it might achieve victory in its wars. In a set of engagingly written cases, Rovner shows how this relationship has often proved elusive, and how ignoring it has frequently proved self-destructive.'
*Barry Posen, Ford International Professor of Political Science, Massachusetts Institute of Technology*

'Joshua Rovner's sharply observed and lucidly argued book is a plea for greater intellectual clarity and self-awareness in Western foreign policy. In today's era, the differences between conventional military strategy and the whole of society effort that is grand strategy need to be properly understood.'
*John Bew, Defence and Security Advisor to the Prime Minister (UK) and Professor of History and Foreign Policy, King's College London*

'Grand strategy and strategy are routinely confused, if not conflated. Exploring both classical and contemporary examples, *Strategy and Grand Strategy* is one of the rare books that carefully untangles the two concepts and asks hard questions about the consequences when leaders mistake them for each other.'
*Thierry Balzacq, Professor of International Relations and Professorial Fellow, Sciences Po*

'Spanning two thousand years of history, Joshua Rovner's new work delineates the often-confused concepts of strategy and grand strategy and substantially advances our understanding of both. This is an important book.'
*Michael C. Horowitz, Richard Perry Professor, University of Pennsylvania; former Deputy Assistant Secretary of Defense for Force Development and Emerging Capabilities (US)*

# Strategy and Grand Strategy

Joshua Rovner

IISS  The International Institute for Strategic Studies

# The International Institute for Strategic Studies

Arundel House | 6 Temple Place | London | WC2R 2PG | UK

First published January 2025 by **Routledge**
4 Park Square, Milton Park, Abingdon, Oxon, OX14 4RN

for **The International Institute for Strategic Studies**
Arundel House, 6 Temple Place, London, WC2R 2PG, UK
www.iiss.org

Simultaneously published in the USA and Canada by **Routledge**
52 Vanderbilt Avenue, New York, NY 10017

*Routledge is an imprint of Taylor & Francis, an Informa Business*

© 2025 The International Institute for Strategic Studies

DIRECTOR-GENERAL AND CHIEF EXECUTIVE Dr Bastian Giegerich
SERIES EDITOR Dr Benjamin Rhode
ASSISTANT EDITOR Gráinne Lucey-Tremblay
EDITORIAL Alice Aveson, Gregory Brooks, Jill Lally, Gráinne Lucey-Tremblay, Christopher Harder
PRODUCTION Alessandra Beluffi, Ravi Gopar, Charlotte Gurr, Jade Panganiban, James Parker, Kelly Verity
COVER ARTWORK Adaptation of James Gillray, *The Times, Anno 1783*. (Photo by Hulton Archive/ Getty Images)

**The International Institute for Strategic Studies** is an independent centre for research, information and debate on the problems of conflict, however caused, that have, or potentially have, an important military content. The Council and Staff of the Institute are international and its membership is drawn from almost 100 countries. The Institute is independent and it alone decides what activities to conduct. It owes no allegiance to any government, any group of governments or any political or other organisation. The IISS stresses rigorous research with a forward-looking policy orientation and places particular emphasis on bringing new perspectives to the strategic debate.

The Institute's publications are designed to meet the needs of a wider audience than its own membership and are available on subscription, by mail order and in good bookshops. Further details at www.iiss.org.

All rights reserved. No part of this book may be reprinted or reproduced or utilised in any form or by any electronic, mechanical or other means, now known or hereafter invented, including photocopying and recording, or in any information storage or retrieval system, without permission in writing from the publishers.

British Library Cataloguing in Publication Data
A catalogue record for this book is available from the British Library

Library of Congress Cataloging in Publication Data

ADELPHI series
ISSN 1944-5571

ADELPHI AP514–515
ISBN 978-1-041-02004-2 / eB 978-1-003-61730-3

# Contents

AUTHOR

**Joshua Rovner** is an Associate Professor of International Relations in the School of International Service at American University. He previously served as the John Goodwin Tower Distinguished Chair in International Politics and National Security at SMU, and as a professor of strategy and policy at the US Naval War College. In 2018–19 he served as scholar-in-residence at the National Security Agency and US Cyber Command. Rovner is the author of *Fixing the Facts: National Security and the Politics of Intelligence* (Cornell University Press, 2011), and the co-editor of *Chaos in the Liberal Order: The Trump Presidency and International Politics in the 21st Century* (Columbia University Press, 2018) and *Chaos Reconsidered: The Liberal Order and the Future of International Politics* (Columbia University Press, 2023).

# ACKNOWLEDGEMENTS

The ideas in this book began as lectures at the US Naval War College. I remain grateful to students and colleagues in the Strategy & Policy Department for their feedback. I would also like to thank participants in seminars at the MIT Security Studies Program; the University of Chicago Program on International Security Policy; the Yale University Brady-Johnson Program on Grand Strategy; the Johns Hopkins University Kissinger Center for Global Affairs; the George Washington University Institute for Security and Conflict Studies; the Boston University Pardee School of Global Studies; the University of Denver Korbel School of International Studies; the University of Indiana Center on American and Global Security; the University of California Washington Center; Peking University; Keio University; RMIT University; the Sejong Institute; the US Naval Postgraduate School; US Cyber Command; the National Nuclear Security Administration; and the Office of Net Assessment in the US Department of Defense. For helpful criticism, I thank Aaron Bateman, Frank Gavin, Brendan Green, Phil Haun, Jon Lindsay, Sergei Radchenko, Iskander Rehman, Caitlin Talmadge, Jana Wattenberg and anonymous reviewers. Ikyhun Lee, Ido Levy and Ian Reynolds provided expert research assistance. Thanks, finally, to the outstanding team at IISS, including Gráinne Lucey-Tremblay, Ravi Gopar, Ulrike Haessler, Jill Lally and Jack May. Benjamin Rhode shepherded the project from its early stages and Alice Aveson saw it to the finish line.

# Two theories

War is a deeply emotional business. The combination of politics and violence triggers intense feelings for all involved. Winning is a source of genuine elation and national pride. Losing a war leads to resentment and, for some, a desperate need for revenge. Mortal danger inspires fear and anger. For civilians caught in the middle, the experience can evoke horror and a dreadful sort of awe. And for those involved in the fighting itself, war is a cauldron of clashing emotions, mixing boredom and anxiety, loneliness and camaraderie, terror and exhilaration.

But perhaps the most curious response to war is bewilderment. It is remarkable how often participants in war seem totally puzzled by the experience. This is particularly odd, given that war requires a huge amount of organisation. We might expect that a set of agreed principles is needed for such an effort; these principles should mitigate confusion. In addition, violence concentrates the mind, especially when national security is on the line. Everyone involved has a compelling reason to understand the strategic logic of war, and the relationship between wartime decisions and the nature of the post-war peace. Yet this is frequently not the case.

Winners often wonder why they cannot translate their wartime victory into durable gains. Losers wonder why they lost. Policymakers wonder why they entered into war without a coherent strategy, and why it is hard to stop fighting. Soldiers wonder why they were sent.

One source of confusion has to do with two distinct but inter-related concepts: strategy and grand strategy. These terms are similar and often used interchangeably. But they are not synon-ymous, and the differences matter. Mistaking strategy for grand strategy is a pathway to frustration for soldiers and statesmen alike. Misunderstanding how they are related is another.

* * *

Strategy is a theory of victory. It explains how to use force in order to achieve political objectives in war. Strategic questions focus on enduring dilemmas about where to send military forces, how much violence to use and when to stop. Many issues stem from these fundamental questions: the role of civilians in war, the economics of mobilisation, the relationship between policymakers and generals, the role of secret intelligence in open combat and the challenges of wartime diplomacy.[1]

A decent strategy tells a plausible story about military violence and state objectives. In doing so it explains how something inher-ently destructive will lead to something politically constructive. Understanding the political logic of force is vital if war is to be anything more than a meaningless spasm of violence. In addition, a good strategy will be reasonably straightforward. Leaders who begin with baroque strategies risk losing focus amid the chaos and confusion of conflict. Finally, it will give leaders the chance to manage the interaction with one or more thinking enemies.

Strategy is inherently interactive as both sides actively try to undermine the other, and both try to anticipate and pre-empt enemy action.

Grand strategy is a theory of security. It explains how to make oneself safe in an unsafe world. It answers questions of what kind of military forces to buy, where to send them and when to use them. Grand strategy also discusses how to coordinate military, diplomatic and economic instruments of national power in order to produce durable national security. If strategy is about winning the war, then grand strategy is about winning the peace.[2]

A decent grand strategy starts with clear assumptions about how the world works. For example, if leaders believe that international politics is more peaceful as democracy spreads, then they ought to invest heavily in pro-democracy movements, support nascent democratic governments and intervene militarily on the side of democratic forces. If they doubt these assumptions, however, then they must choose a different approach. Beyond first principles, a grand strategy must be able to distinguish real security problems from phantom threats and prioritise resources accordingly. Finally, a viable grand strategy must calibrate available resources with national objectives and coordinate different instruments of national power to achieve them. Above all it must guard against wishful thinking about ends and means.

Even a thoughtful grand strategy does not guarantee long-term security, however. This is especially true if it requires occasional fighting. It is possible to enter war for the right reasons only to lose it all through strategic blunders. Bad wartime decisions squander lives and resources; they erode public faith; and they potentially leave the state vulnerable to third parties who may take advantage of their misfortune. The cost of recovering may exceed the value of the political object at stake.

It is also possible to conduct an outstanding wartime campaign in the service of a deeply flawed grand strategy.

Military leaders can design and execute brilliant plans to force the enemy to capitulate, even if the long-term security benefit is negligible. Worse, the happy memory of strategic triumph may obscure the fact that intervention was a costly diversion at best, which makes it possible that states will repeat their mistakes. Some wars are not worth fighting even if they are well fought.

These basic ideas lead to some unsettling paradoxes: sometimes winning in war is bad for the state, especially if it encourages more investment in conflicts of marginal importance for national security. The good work of generals will prove counterproductive if strategic success obscures deeper problems in grand strategy. It is easy to indulge in military triumphalism in the afterglow of victory and put aside questions about the long-term viability of a state's theory of security. The converse is also true: sometimes losing is necessary for grand strategy. Wartime failures are important if they force leaders to have difficult discussions about the real sources of security, and if they undermine the pernicious effects of military nostalgia.

All of this is peculiar. In its ideal form, strategy is a linear process in which military violence leads to some political goal. We think of grand strategy in comparable terms. Barry Posen's famous definition, for example, explains that grand strategy is a 'political–military means–ends chain, a state's theory about how it can best "cause" security for itself'.[3] Success in both cases depends on the degree to which strategists and grand strategists are able to sustain a predictable approach. Strategies that cannot show how violence will produce some political change will probably fail. Grand strategies that cannot describe the logical link between national effort and national security are vacuous. Yet these linear, logical, common-sense arguments about successful strategy and grand strategy break down when we explore the relationship between them. When common sense loses traction, bewilderment follows.

*   *   *

Exploring the relationship between strategy and grand strategy reveals other curious historical patterns. It tells us, for instance, something unexpected about deterrence.

Durable national security sometimes relies on mutual restraint. Peace should obtain when the balance of military capabilities is such that rivals cannot defeat one another. Mutually assured denial ought to be particularly stable in cases of cross-domain deterrence, that is, when each rival dominates a particular war-fighting domain (e.g., land, sea or air). Great powers with comparative advantages in one domain should avoid fighting great powers who are superior in another. Having no obvious way of overcoming their disadvantages, they should default to peace, because going to war would put their military forces in danger and put their grand strategies at terrific risk. Yet they have done so repeatedly. Why?

Part of the reason is the hubris that comes with grand-strategic success. Great powers grow secure and prosperous by cultivating their capabilities in a preferred domain. But success breeds ambition, and it encourages the belief that they can break out of existing power balances through will-power and cleverness. Ambitious rising great powers are more likely to pick fights with rivals, even when those rivals are clearly superior in other domains. They are also more likely to embrace long-shot strategic approaches that promise quick and decisive victory without having to confront their enemy's centre of gravity. This sequence of events can end in strategic disaster.

Such was the case in the Peloponnesian War, which I explore in Chapter One. Athens had become wealthy and powerful in the fifth century BCE by constructing a naval trading empire. It poured resources into its navy, which it then used to expand trade routes and establish a system of colonies and tributary allies. All of this would be of little use in a war against Sparta, however, given the latter's dominant army. Sparta's grand strategy, in contrast, was geographically conservative. It needed to keep its army close to home to protect against external threats and to prevent a slave uprising on the Peloponnese. Over the years Sparta developed technologies and tactics for maximising the combat power of its heavy infantry and won universal acclaim as the strongest land power in ancient Greece. Like Athens, it had slowly implemented a viable and durable grand strategy. Also like Athens, it could not militarily compete outside its preferred domain.

They tried anyway. Athens and Sparta were not blind to the balance of power before the war, yet they convinced themselves that they could work around it. Athens tried to lure Sparta to fight at sea; Sparta tried to lure Athens to fight on land. These attempts failed. Both sides retreated from their early-war fantasies, but neither was willing to make peace. What followed was a grinding conflict with little prospect of decisive battle, an exhausting process that undermined their respective theories of security. Athens and Sparta were deterred from attacking one another's centre of gravity, and as a result they consigned themselves to protracted war.

We may see this story again soon. The United States, the dominant global maritime power, is increasingly at loggerheads with China, the dominant power on land in East Asia.

Both countries have invested in specific military capabilities designed to undermine their rivals without having to attack in the other's preferred domain. They have also published doctrinal statements that offer the alluring prospect of victory through rapid electronic and information attacks. Such strategies hold out for seizing the initiative and forcing the adversary to capitulate without having to risk a large-scale engagement. Should these fail, however, both sides might find themselves stuck much like the ancients were stuck, committed to war but lacking the ability to win quickly. Novel strategic concepts might undo each great power's grand strategy.

In 1778 France entered the American War of Independence, providing vital material support to the impoverished Americans. Yet French assistance went far beyond simply providing ships, soldiers and cash. Working with their American counterparts, French military leaders developed an effective strategy for overcoming British strength. French–American coordination, an exceptional synthesis of naval and land power, remains a model of both coalition warfare and joint operations. Planners carefully tailored military action to achieve shared political objectives, ultimately forcing Great Britain to concede defeat.

What happened next was a calamity. Waging war effectively with ragtag American troops required a huge investment in money and material. In the short term France benefited from bloodying its long-time rival and forcing it to abandon a prized colony. But it incurred an enormous debt in the process, pushing the government towards bankruptcy. This in turn kicked off the extraordinary chain of events leading to the French Revolution and the destruction of the monarchy.

Events played out very differently on the other side of the Channel. British strategists made a series of critical mistakes that enabled the French and American victory. The Royal Navy missed opportunities to attack and perhaps demolish key elements of the French fleet that were vital for sustaining the American cause. Britain's army suffered from miscommunication and disunity of effort, problems that plagued the early war efforts to destroy continental forces in the northern half of the country. British commanders also blundered badly in the south, leading to the shocking surrender at Yorktown, a loss that effectively ended the war. British strategy in the war was a dismal failure.

After the shooting stopped, however, Great Britain resumed its imperial expansion and the march towards hegemony. Losing the colonies forced it to rethink the value of maintaining a large standing army in North America, and it rid it of colonial troublemakers, who were increasingly unwilling to accept royal rule. For Britain, losing the war was a blessing: instead of policing vast territories full of hostile colonists, it could reinvest in its navy, hold onto the colonies that it needed and strike deals with others for port access and resupply. It returned to practising the art of offshore balancing, spending more than a century maintaining the naval dominance that underwrote its position as the hub of international trade and finance, while cultivating great-power allies in Europe who would do the heavy lifting if any state attempted to conquer the continent. The strategic debacle in the American war brought a grand-strategic reassessment that led to a period of astonishing wealth and power.

French strategic success led to grand-strategic disaster. British strategic failure led to a lasting grand-strategic triumph. Chapter Two explores these surprising outcomes in detail. The French and British experiences deserve special attention because no other historical case puts these strategy–grand strategy distinctions in such stark relief. And no other case better reveals the dangers of mistaking one for the other.

\*   \*   \*

Strategy and grand strategy also help us interpret more recent history, as I discuss in Chapter Three. Major controversies from the Cold War turn on these concepts. Criticism of US strategy in the Vietnam War, for example, has long focused on the military's preference for conventional operations. Instead of engaging in a thoroughgoing counter-insurgency campaign, say critics, it chose a tragically ill-suited war of attrition. But the problems in Vietnam were not really the result of combat preferences. The real issue was the lack of an intelligible grand strategy during the period of its major combat operations, in the years between the Cuban Missile Crisis and detente. The fact that grand strategy was in flux made it impossible to settle on a definition of victory. While the main objective was the preservation of an independent non-communist South Vietnam, there was no consensus about how to know when Saigon could stand on its own. Or, more precisely, there was no agreement about the consequences of Saigon's possible collapse. There was also no consensus on how to apply enough US force to compel North Vietnam to negotiate, while simultaneously weaning South Vietnam off the US security guarantee. Without a clear idea of US grand strategy, policymakers could not settle on the value of the object in the war.

The result was a set of related problems plaguing US strategy. The lack of consensus about political goals led to confusion and doubt about appropriate measures of progress. It also led to hedging and half-hearted proposals from leaders who were not sure what they wanted. Grand-strategic ambiguity deepened fissures among officials from across the national-security establishment, civilian and military alike, all of whom went to war with their own beliefs about the best course of action. Policymakers opted for self-contradictory strategies as they tried to mediate these disputes, making concessions to all the major players rather than choosing winners and losers. About the only thing that military and political leaders shared was frustration about the outcome.

The Vietnam War was nested within the larger Cold War between the superpowers, and nuclear weapons loomed over their rivalry. The value of nuclear weapons in the Cold War divided observers, then and now. Scholars adhering to the 'nuclear revolution' thesis have long argued that the weapons were too powerful to use. The weapons were so destructive that it was impossible to calibrate violent means with political ends. Indeed, the notion of 'victory' was absurd because any nuclear use invited retaliation in kind. Nuclear weapons were only useful for deterrence, and even that was difficult. This idea influenced scholarship on issues ranging from diplomacy and arms control to crisis stability and the problem of misperception.

But US leaders never embraced the revolution. Instead of viewing nuclear weapons solely as tools of deterrence, they invested in technologies to reduce the cost of war. They hoped that more accurate warheads could target enemy forces without threatening enemy cities. Better intelligence and surveillance might allow the US to take out enemy nuclear forces at the outset of any war. And as cost-reduction scenarios became plausible, deterrent threats would become more credible, improving everyone's security.

The theory of the nuclear revolution also failed to explain leaders' fear of proliferation. If nuclear weapons were great for deterrence but lousy for battle, then Washington should have been sanguine as the technology spread. It might even have been optimistic, since proliferation would, under the theory, lead countries to become cautious. Instead, US leaders worried that the spread of nuclear weapons would spin out of control, and they spent decades trying to prevent it.

Strategy and grand strategy provide a way of reconciling these arguments. The nuclear-revolution thesis does not appear to pass the historical test in terms of grand strategy. If the nuclear revolution affected grand strategy, the US should have settled for a small arsenal for the sole purpose of deterrence. It should have abandoned efforts to integrate nuclear and conventional forces. US leaders should have recognised that defences against nuclear attack were futile. And they should have managed the process of proliferation so that states, both great and regional powers alike, enjoyed the security benefit of a reliable second-strike capability. None of these things happened.

The theory fares better at the level of strategy. While nuclear weapons have not changed everything, one critical fact remains: no state has used them in anger since 1945. States have been perfectly willing to use other novel military technologies on the battlefield, suggesting that there is something abnormal about these weapons that changes how leaders think about them. Cold War leaders blanched when confronted with operational plans for nuclear use. And in crises they stepped back from the brink, over and over. Leaders were not willing to take the kind of risks with nuclear weapons that they took with conventional military forces – precisely what the nuclear-revolution thesis predicts.

The nuclear dilemma is not a Cold War anachronism, as the persistent debates over nuclear weapons attest. The strategy–grand strategy framework provides a new way of understanding current controversies. Today's nuclear hawks argue that policy should not be constrained by a theory that fails at the level of grand strategy. From their perspective, the arsenal provides a number of important benefits to US foreign policy beyond its utility in wartime. But for more cautious critics, the strategic level matters most. If there is no rational argument for using nuclear weapons in anger, then there is little to be gained from posturing with them for other purposes. The risks of wartime catastrophe far outweigh the marginal peacetime benefits of a larger force.

* * *

Strategy and grand strategy shed light on other contemporary controversies, including counter-terrorism. The war on terrorism posed an immediate challenge to strategists after 9/11, because the endgame was unclear. US officials wanted to destroy al-Qaeda, not coerce it into some negotiated settlement. But what it meant to destroy a transnational organisation was up for debate, not least because any militant group could claim the al-Qaeda banner after Osama bin Laden and his cohort were dispatched. As a result, the strategic goal was nebulous.

Grand strategy helped bring the US counter-terrorism approach into focus, as I explain in Chapter Four. The goal of grand strategy is security, which is a general condition rather than a specific objective. Victory was not the point. Instead, counter-terrorism sought to reduce the risk of violence at a sustainable cost. Over four administrations, the US gradually transformed its 'global war on terrorism' into something more like air policing, the British approach to imperial control in the Middle East and North Africa in the interwar period. Rather than requiring large land forces to garrison distant countries, it envisioned the use of special-operations forces, intelligence and drone strikes for what it called over-the-horizon strikes. This vision did not imagine an end state, just as there is no moment in which police can declare victory over crime. Even withdrawals from war zones do not mean the end of counter-terrorism; the US has continued to conduct operations with great energy since exiting Afghanistan.

*   *   *

Future conflicts will include emerging technologies that raise the possibility of radical changes to the conduct of war. States are already incorporating novel tools like malicious code and artificial intelligence (AI) in their conventional military forces. According to some observers, the ability to operate in new domains like cyberspace might give first movers a dramatic advantage. The ability to operate effectively in the digital domain will allow forces to coordinate efforts over vast distances in real time. The ability to disrupt and disable others' communications through cyberspace might prevent the enemy from organising a successful defence. The upshot is a vision of rapid, low-casualty conflict, where the outcome is determined not by who controls territory but by who controls information flows.

This is not the first time that states have pondered the implications of war in new domains. Seventeenth-century naval technologies opened the blue-water oceans for trade as well as battle. Contemporaneous observers argued that naval mastery would confer outsize political power, because control of sea lanes would allow states to dominate commerce and set the terms of naval engagements. At the same time, they worried that failure to rapidly develop and field capital ships would put

the state in a position of permanent inferiority to more technologically savvy rivals. Over time, however, observers learned
the limits of naval technology. Their existential concerns gave
way to more modest expectations. The same pattern of hope,
fear and resignation describes the experience of observers at
the dawn of strategic bombing in the interwar period, as well
as the dawn of the space age.

Interestingly, the pattern holds for both strategy and grand
strategy, as I argue in Chapter Five. Strategists in all these transitional periods imagined that wars in new domains would be
short and decisive. They urged leaders to exploit the advantages that new technologies offered and warned them about
the dangers of procrastination. Grand strategists made similar
arguments about operating in new domains. Control of sea
lanes opened up an avenue for durable security, and relin-
quishing control meant open-ended insecurity. Airpower
theorists also called for investments in large bomber fleets and
dedicated air forces, not just to win wars but also to deter any
potential challengers from starting them.

If this history is a useful guide, then the current rhetoric
is probably ahead of reality. Those who seek to fight in new
domains will struggle to operationalise new concepts, not least
because they need skilled personnel who are in high demand
in the private sector. Recruiting and retaining these professionals will be difficult because firms offer the potential for higher
salaries, better benefits and more flexibility. Organisational
performance will also lag behind technological promises because
of bureaucratic friction. Integrating advanced data and communications systems into conventional operations requires the kind
of coordination that will prove difficult to sustain, especially
in wartime. More importantly, fierce competition among rival
states foreshadows a cat-and-mouse contest as offensive innovations lead to defensive responses. Technological advantages

may be important, but they will not endure. At some point states will have a better sense of the uses and limits of cyberspace operations and AI-powered information offensives.

But we have not yet reached that point. The great powers are competing aggressively for technology advantages, and their leaders are not lowering expectations. Instead, they are urging innovation and warning about the dangers of falling behind. They see a future in which national security is inseparable from information security. Economic prosperity relies on secure and reliable financial transactions; social stability relies on robust and resilient infrastructure; and military capability relies on information technologies built into weapons systems and on communications networks that coordinate fielded forces. Modern great powers believe earnestly that the quality of grand strategy rests on the mastery of advanced technologies. They believe the same about strategy in future wars, and they worry openly about nightmare scenarios, of sudden and overwhelming losses to savvier enemies.

Such fears will probably lessen over time. The problem in the interim period, however, is a wicked mix of enthusiasm and alarm. Great powers that fixate on technology are likely to choose strategies based on visions of short conflicts where the outcome is a function of relative technological sophistication. They are also likely to believe that the outcome will determine the state's security long after the war is over. These beliefs inspire a sense of urgency to planning, because while there is a possibility for a quick and decisive victory, there is little margin for error. The reality of war, of course, might be very different. Offensive technologies can fail under fire, and defenders may adapt in novel and unexpected ways. Military leaders under these circumstances might scramble to adjust their theories of victory – if they do not jettison them entirely. Pre-war strategic assumptions often fall apart when the shooting starts, a pattern well known to military historians and war fighters alike. Less well understood is the curious and counter-intuitive relationship between strategy and grand strategy. That is the subject of this book.

## CHAPTER ONE

# Strategy and grand strategy in the Peloponnesian War

Athens and Sparta boasted excellent grand strategies before the Peloponnesian War (431–404 BCE), and both were poised to enjoy a long period of security based on mutual deterrence. Athens dominated the sea; Sparta dominated the land. Yet each side lost confidence in its theory of security in the years before the war, and they came to believe that fighting was necessary and right. Losing faith in grand strategy posed a real problem for strategy, however, because Athens had no obvious method of overcoming the Spartan army, and Sparta had no clear path to victory against the Athenian fleet. Sensing that war was inevitable but lacking good ideas about how to win it, the great powers embraced strategic fantasies. Both convinced themselves that they could win quickly – and without challenging their enemy on its preferred domain. Painful wartime experiences disabused them of these delusions, leading to more cautious strategies and a very long war. Mutual deterrence, which had disappeared before the war, returned with a vengeance after the fighting began. The price was a protracted conflict that exhausted both great powers.

Strategy and grand strategy help explain this famous Greek disaster. Leaders on both sides crafted coherent theories of security but were unable to stop their colleagues from making wartime choices that put those theories at risk. Highly respected Spartans and Athenians made impressive arguments in favour of the status quo before the war. Caution made sense, but it wasn't terribly appealing for great powers on the make. Men of ambition on both sides made the case for war, even though the available strategic options were not consistent with their broader grand strategies. For most Athenians and Spartans, there was nothing glorious about the status quo.[1]

The case also tells us something important about deterrence. Two great powers faced off in antiquity, one dominant on land and the other dominant at sea. We might have expected a long period of stability, given that their comparative advantages made them largely invulnerable to attack. This situation, what modern international-relations theorists call cross-domain deterrence, ought to produce at least a grudging peace. But although ancient Spartans and Athenians accurately recognised the balance, they still went to war. Contemporary analyses have likewise addressed the cross-domain balance between China and the United States in East Asia. Now, as then, each side maintains superior capabilities in its preferred domain. Now, as then, the great powers are drifting closer to conflict. Does the collapse of deterrence in ancient Greece foreshadow a similar disaster today? And is there anything they can do about it?

*   *   *

Geography conditioned the grand strategies of the ancient Greek great powers. Athens would have probably remained a modest agricultural community if not for access to the protected port at Piraeus, which provided a basis for maritime trade.

Key Athenian officials grasped the possibilities for security and prosperity in the early fifth century BCE, using their naval power to build a growing constellation of colonies and tributary allies. Maintaining control over this sprawling and unwieldy empire was a practical problem, requiring continued investment in the kind of navy that could patrol vast distances and the kind of administrative structure that could organise the complex finances and logistics of maritime power. The Aegean Sea created both opportunities and headaches.

Sparta enjoyed a much larger and defensible position on the Peloponnese and set about developing its strength on land. It famously organised its society around the creation and maintenance of heavy infantry. Spartan citizens spent their lives practising phalanx warfare, and they relied on a large slave population to give them the time to concentrate exclusively on martial affairs. This arrangement, however, created its own risks. The fear of a slave uprising constrained Spartan grand strategy: sending the army on long journeys abroad was a recipe for disaster. In this sense Sparta's problem was the opposite of Athens'. If Athens worried about rebellions in distant places, Sparta worried about maintaining control at home.

Both great powers crafted grand strategies that suited their particular geographic, economic, political and diplomatic needs. Athens built a naval trading empire that delivered revenue into the treasury, which it then used to build more and better warships. The need to project power over long distances also put a premium on skilled crews and better technology. Impressive innovations in ship design increased the range, reliability and combat power in battle. Equally impressive innovations in logistics, maintenance, storage and accounting made Athens' navy the institutional bedrock of its grand strategy. Heroic naval battles may have occupied poets and scribes, but Athens' golden era was also a triumph of bureaucracy.

Athens' rise began long before the Peloponnesian War. Its theory of security emerged early in the fifth century BCE, when it began to transition from a middling agrarian city-state to a naval trading empire. Historians credit the Athenian leader Themistocles for spearheading this change and overcoming the scepticism of many of his colleagues. Critically, he convinced the assembly to invest the profits from a newly discovered silver mine in a large navy, and to start building the infrastructure for sustaining the fleet. Ships were not enough: a naval strategy would require port facilities and shipyards, woodworking and metalworking workshops, and enormous warehouses. It would also require tax reforms and novel forms of public–private financing. His naval programme was coherent and sustainable, as was the Athenian grand strategy on which it was based, but it asked a lot from its logisticians.[2]

Its approach also raised difficult political questions. Maintaining access to distant outposts required not just a navy but also a reliable network of coastal outposts, and this meant dealing with a patchwork of local polities. Athens could gain access through conquest or by diplomatic arrangement; in either case, observers were bound to worry about its growing power. By the start of the war the Delian League boasted about 150 members. Some were more enthusiastic than others.[3]

Athenian leaders worried that the elaborate network could fall apart, and that rivals could exploit fissures in the League. Indeed, the flashpoint for the Peloponnesian War was civil unrest in a distant backwater called Epidamnus, a tiny outpost on the edge of the Greek world (now modern-day Albania). Ordinarily this would not have roused the Athenians, because Epidamnus itself was not important for Athenian security or prosperity. But their smaller allies warned that losing the colony to a pro-Spartan faction would set in motion a cascade of defections, ultimately putting Athens at risk. Ambition and anxiety came together in ancient Athens;

the same combination characterises modern rising great powers, as we will see in later chapters. For all of its impressive gains, Athenian officials could not abide minor losses. Above all they worried that colonies and tributary allies would rebel against the League, hollowing out Athens' influence from the inside, and that third parties would encourage this corrosive trend. Increasing the size of the League gave them more to worry about. Paradoxically, Athens felt less secure as its relative power grew.

Yet for all these practical and political problems, Athens' grand strategy was coherent and sustainable. The aggressive expansion of maritime trade made it rich. Pouring those riches back into the navy allowed it to expand further, setting off a virtuous cycle of power and prosperity. Contributing to Athens' naval expeditions conferred social status on wealthy Athenians, encouraging them to give more. And the growth of the navy inspired an administrative revolution that linked economic gains with power projection.

By the time the war began in 431 BCE, Athens could boast a fleet of 300 triremes along with an elaborate supporting infra-structure at Piraeus. Sustaining the fleet was a bureaucratic and economic triumph, given the cost and complexity of the trireme itself: an elaborate three-tiered rowing galley designed for speed and close combat. Athenian ships were engineer-ing marvels, but they were difficult to build and maintain, and Athenian leaders had to balance the total size of the navy against the practical limits of material fatigue, storage facilities and ship repair.[4] They also faced a familiar trade-off between procurement and readiness. A larger fleet would have required a much greater investment in personnel, and rowers did not come cheap. Experienced ship crews were essential to trireme operations, which demanded a combination of precision, forti-tude under stress and raw endurance. The life of a rower was difficult, dangerous and very unpleasant. Rowers, reasonably enough, demanded appropriate compensation.[5]

Athenian officials were not blind to these problems and understood the economic risks of a prolonged war. So, they planned to fight a short one. A war lasting more than three years would exhaust its war chest, at which point it would have to demand a good deal more in tribute from allies and taxes from its own citizens. In extremis it could melt down gold statues to cover ship losses and pay crews, and plead with private citizens to sponsor new triremes. Ultimately it would have to take all these steps, as the war dragged on much longer than anyone expected.[6]

But these hard times were difficult to imagine at the outset of the war. Athens was confident it could win quickly, not least because its navy was so far ahead of those of the other Hellenic powers. Corinth and Corcyra could maintain fleets about a third of the size of Athens'.[7] Sparta could also muster about 100 ships, but it lacked competent ship captains, rowers and steersmen.[8] Sparta's political economy was ill-suited for continuous maritime operations. Its only serviceable port was 30 miles from the capital, and it did not possess anything like Athens' supporting infrastructure. Spartan males almost exclusively joined the army, making it difficult to fill out ship crews. Making matters worse, Sparta used deliberately inconvenient iron spits rather than coins for its currency, given its belief that coinage was corrupting. This made it difficult to attract mercenary rowers.[9]

Sparta's naval weakness was not a sign of irrationality. Quite the opposite: its focus on land made perfect sense given its grand-strategic priorities. Because Sparta never took its navy seriously, it could spend the bulk of its resources fielding the largest army in Greece, which may have been three times the size of Athens' army.[10] Because Spartan citizens understood their security ultimately rested on land power, they could devote themselves to learning the art of heavy-infantry warfare and perfecting phalanx tactics from an early age. Endless drilling taught them to work collectively and obey orders, which helped command-ers choreograph rapid manoeuvres even in the confusion of battle. Spartan hoplites earned a reputation for battlefield courage and ruthlessness.

Effectiveness in ground combat was essential because Sparta's grand strategy focused close to home. Its theory of security was that a dominant army could fend off Argos, its main enemy on land. As the army grew in power and prestige, the smaller Arcadian cities on the Peloponnese would have no choice but to bandwagon with Sparta. By focusing on peninsular security rather than projecting power abroad, the Spartan army could deter the slave population from rebelling. And as long as the army stayed close to home, it would not have to reform its peculiar economy. The division of labour among citizens and slaves was simple and sustainable, and it served as the bedrock for what might have been an enduring period of stability. The radical changes that had transformed Athens were unnecessary in Sparta, a fundamentally conservative great power.[11]

Athens and Sparta pursued very different grand strategies, built upon different geographic and economic foundations. Yet both sides built military forces that reflected their underlying ideas of security, investing in their comparative advantages and sacrificing other capabilities. For Athens, this meant build-ing a dominant navy and downplaying its agrarian hoplite tradition. For Sparta, this meant building a dominant army and treating sea power as an afterthought.

\* \* \*

The cross-domain military balance was obvious when the fighting began. Athens ruled the seas but not the land.

Sparta's army could defeat the whole of Greece in a single battle, as the Athenian leader Pericles admitted, but it had a modest and ineffective navy.[12] Both great powers thought about money, diplomacy and force in terms of their relative strengths. Each had constructed coherent grand strategies, and they had the ability to defend against their strongest rival. This state of affairs – a military balance between two states who had no interest in challenging each other directly – should have been sustainable. Why did it fall apart?[13]

The answer to that question is complex and contested. Indeed, the debate over the origins of the Peloponnesian War is a famously divisive issue for scholars and strategists, and I cannot do it justice here. The fraught diplomacy of the pre-war years clearly played an important role, however, not least because it caused Athens and Sparta to worry about the foundations of their grand strategies. Smaller states warned that cross-domain stability was tenuous and that shifting alliances threatened to upset the military balance. They urged Athens and Sparta to take a more active role in distant political affairs rather than letting their power atrophy by allowing countervailing alliances to form against them. Foreign crises thus became proxy contests, which created more opportunities for direct military confrontation. Increasingly convinced that they faced existential threats, the great powers scrambled for psychologically comforting arguments about how to use force. These strategic arguments were foolhardy, as they soon learned. The consequence was a long, ruinous war, the impoverishment of the Hellenic great powers and the end of Greece's golden age.

The prelude to the war was the crisis between Corcyra and Corinth, who were at loggerheads in the Epidamnus affair and heading towards war. Corinth had engaged in a naval buildup in 433–432, causing Corcyra to petition Athens for protection and for a place in the Delian League. Corcyra was clearly motivated by self-interest, to be sure, but it also played on Athenian anxiety about losing its naval edge. Corcyran delegates presented an ominous scenario. If Corinth was able to defeat Corcyra, it could merge their navies into a combined fleet perhaps two-thirds the size of Athens' own. And if it took that fleet to the Peloponnesian League, as was likely, then Sparta could achieve maritime numerical parity with Athens. The loss of naval mastery would not only threaten Athens' chances in a future war but also undermine the foundations of its grand strategy.

Corinth responded. Fearful that its main adversary would secure an alliance with Athens, it turned to Sparta. Mindful of Athens' growing power, it warned Sparta that if it did not expand its alliances it would become 'weaker and less terrifying to a strengthened enemy'.[14] The Delian League would gain a stranglehold on maritime commerce if Athens was able to add the Corinthian and Corcyran fleets. Their combined strength would enable it to threaten supplies of grain to the Peloponnese, especially if Athens could control the narrow land bridge separating the peninsula from mainland Greece. On the other hand, a combined Peloponnesian League fleet would strengthen deterrence and bolster Sparta's position. The Corinthians reasoned that Athens would be more cautious in the face of a stronger naval adversary, given the risks involved. As the Corinthians put it, 'a single defeat at sea is in all likelihood their ruin'.[15]

Athens and Sparta had spent decades focusing on their comparative military strengths, and the result was a durable cross-domain balance. Now the middle-sized powers in the ancient Greek world were warning that it could all come undone unless they intervened more aggressively in a distant conflict among third parties. Not all observers believed that the military balance was fragile, however, or that war made much sense. Sparta's King Archidamus, for example, offered a remarkably prescient forecast to the Spartan assembly during the crisis. Archidamus inveighed against hubris given military realities. Athens' naval mastery would allow it to open up new theatres of its choosing, which would make it impossible for Sparta to gain the strategic initiative. But he softened these warnings by reminding his colleagues that Sparta's army remained unchallenged and the ultimate guarantor of its sovereignty. War, he argued, was both dangerous and unnecessary. Patience and a methodical accumulation of resources made more sense than a headlong rush into conflict.[16]

Archidamus failed to persuade his impatient colleagues. It is not entirely clear why, though it seems that a mix of hope and fear were fuelling Sparta's hawkish turn. The fear was that a larger Delian League fleet could encircle and strangle the Spartan economy, leaving it in a position of permanent inferiority. The hope was that diplomatic action and military boldness could turn the cross-domain balance in its favour. If Corinth were able to defeat Corcyra, the result would be a Peloponnesian League navy not terribly smaller than Athens'. Meanwhile, Sparta hoped to secure an alliance with Persia, which could provide the resources for a rapid trireme build-up. This was a long shot. At best, such a deal with Persia would make it dependent on the goodwill of a large eastern empire. A more likely scenario was that any such arrangement, if Persia was interested in the first place, would buckle under the logistical burden of maintaining such a large fleet at such distances.

Intense pre-war politics pushed Athenian and Spartan leaders towards superficial analyses of their own grand strategies. This had serious consequences for their strategic choices. Athens obsessed over falling dominoes, fearing that defections from the Delian League would inspire others to follow and put at risk the complex network of partnerships that Athens had formed over several decades. Some worried that such a breakdown would inevitably undermine Athens' economy as well, and thus the underlying source of Athenian power. This encouraged a heavy-handed approach, which added fuel to Spartan propaganda about Athens' imperial ambitions. A more relaxed approach to alliance politics would have served it well, but few in the city were in the mood for patience as the war approached. Preventing any fissures became a fetish, even if the economic consequences were manageable.[17]

Sparta also started questioning the economic foundations of its grand strategy. Its reliance on foreign grain supplies caused it to fear that Athenian naval dominance would make it vulnerable to starvation. Athens might attack grain shipments, confiscating or destroying the cargo and dissuading future deliveries, or it might enact a blockade. In either case, Sparta would face a difficult choice: capitulate to Athenian demands and accept a position of permanent inferiority or send the army abroad to fight Athens and its allies – and risk a slave rebellion on the Peloponnese. But it was not clear that these nightmare scenarios were plausible, or whether Sparta was really so helpless to respond. A careful analysis might have set Sparta at ease. Much like the situation in Athens, though, pre-war Spartan politics did not favour caution or restraint.

\* \* \*

Pericles the Athenian warned about the dangers of rash and self-defeating action. Archidamus the Spartan counselled patience. Both were highly respected leaders and both made their arguments in carefully crafted speeches. Most of their countrymen, however, were convinced by their smaller allies that the balance of power was fragile and that inaction was irresponsible. And while observers on both sides were also well aware of their weaknesses, they thought that their relative weaknesses were not insurmountable. Spartan hawks believed that new allies could deliver critical resources, and that efforts to provoke rebellions could undermine the Athenian empire without having to stare down the Athenian fleet. Likewise, Athenians were tempted by the possibility of open-ended naval mastery though an alliance with Corcyra, which would allow it to coerce Sparta without having to face a Spartan phalanx. Pericles based his strategy on the belief that naval advantages trumped land advantages. A dominant fleet would allow Athens to find new resources, while Sparta, which could hardly project power, faced the risk of starvation and could not fight a long war. Finally, a navy could do more than simply fight other navies because it could deliver and resupply land forces for raiding Spartan allies and stirring up insurrection among the slaves of the Peloponnese. As he put it, 'our naval skill is of more use to us for service on land, than their military skill for service at sea'.[18]

Having decided on war, the great powers turned to questions of strategy, each side hoping to craft strategies that would force the enemy to fight in its preferred domain. Athens' strategy was to stay behind its city walls and use its navy to harass the Peloponnese, instigate a slave rebellion, undermine the Spartan economy, discredit the Spartan war party and force Sparta to admit the impossibility of winning. Sparta's strategy was to invade Attica and ravage the land, baiting the inferior Athenian infantry to come out from behind its city walls and fight a pitched battle.

These strategies failed. Neither Athens nor Sparta took the bait. Both were extremely cautious when it came to facing the enemy on its own terms, and both sides routinely fled rather than fight in an unfamiliar domain. Athens repeatedly tried to lure Sparta into fleet-on-fleet engagements, and Sparta repeatedly tried to bait Athens into pitched battle. Both were frustrated. Cross-domain asymmetries deterred each side from attacking the other's centre of gravity, meaning that they could not engineer the kind of confrontation that might have forced the other to capitulate. At the same time, the political stakes of the war were so high that few were willing to back down, even if a negotiated settlement made sense to everyone. A terrible irony set in. Early war frustrations forced military and political leaders to confront their own weaknesses again, inspiring caution all around. Deterrence returned to the war, and political and military leaders chose to avoid the kind of battles that might have ended it.

The first few years of fighting were pivotal. Both attempted something like what Basil Liddell Hart called the 'indirect approach', with disappointing results.[19] Athens' strategy was based on evacuating Athenians from the countryside and sheltering them behind the city walls, while the navy pressured Sparta by luring its fleet into battle. One problem with this strategy was it transformed the city of Athens into a crowded, oppressive, disease-ridden place, full of distraught citizens who were forced to leave their farms open to the Spartan invaders.

Meanwhile, Sparta hoped that public pressure would compel Athenian leaders to mobilise an army for battle outside the city walls. In other words, it hoped to bait Pericles into abandoning his conservative strategy and fighting on Spartan terms. But Pericles had ways of relieving public pressure without taking the bait. In order to satisfy public desire for action without challenging the Spartans directly, he mobilised a large army – the largest in Athens' history – in a campaign to ravage the land around Sparta's ally Megara. The sight of 10,000 Athenian hoplites in action seems to have inspired his fellow citizens and bought their continued support, but the campaign itself achieved very little and put a huge strain on the treasury.

Sparta suffered the same fate the next year, when it launched a hopeful but ill-conceived amphibious expedition. Like Athens' march to Megara, it sought to attack Athenian allies without confronting Athens' main source of power, and the expedition was predictably futile. Things went from bad to worse for the fledgling Spartan navy in 429, when Athens routed a combined Spartan–Corinthian fleet at Naupactus. The Peloponnesians brought 47 ships to battle against 20 Athenian triremes, but Athenian captains were vastly more experienced and skilled, and the Peloponnesian force fell into disarray at the first sign of trouble. Sparta may have believed that a dramatic naval victory would have destroyed the image of Athenian naval dominance and convinced Persia to enter the war on its side, but Athens' victory reinforced its reputation.[20]

Mutual caution set in after these disappointments, and operational boldness disappeared. Sparta tried to harass Athenian commercial shipping, and Athens tried to encourage slave rebellions. The great powers fought no significant land battles for the first seven years of the war. They fought very few significant naval battles at all. Instead of looking for creative ways to break the balance, both sides retreated to familiar operations. These enabled both sides to continue fighting but prevented either of them from winning. Athens' coastal raiding failed to threaten the Spartan army, which could easily return in the event of a serious slave uprising. Sparta's strategy meanwhile failed to target any of the three main sources of Athenian power: its navy, its alliances and its long walls.[21]

Both sides were also cautious in tactics, repeatedly passing up opportunities for decisive battle on hearing that the enemy was nearby. Tactical retreat became the default position when operating on the other's domain. Spartan captains, for instance, abandoned an uncharacteristically ambitious plan for a surprise naval attack on Piraeus in the winter of 429–428. When Spartan captains heard that Athens was mobilising, they returned to the Peloponnese rather than risking fleet-on-fleet battle. They were especially disheartened because their allies, who were similarly nervous about challenging the Athenian navy, did not honour their promise to support the invasion. Sparta abandoned similar expeditions to Attica (428) and Corcyra (427) when it received word that Athens was preparing a response. It simply could not bear the risk.[22]

Athenian tactics were similar. Occasional land campaigns relied on stealth and trickery and, above all, avoiding pitched battle. Athenian commanders hoped to enter defended cities through bribery and surprise rather than by fighting through Spartan defenders. These plots usually amounted to nothing, however, and Athenian leaders usually withdrew when they heard that Spartans were nearby, as was the case in Corinth (425) and Megara (424).[23] Athens' best shot at a decisive victory on land came at Mantinea (418), when Sparta fought its old peninsular enemy Argos in the largest land battle of the war. Argos and its allies fielded about 12,000 troops on the Peloponnese, while Sparta mobilised as many as 18,000.[24] Despite its numerical weakness, Argos benefited from several tactical advantages, and it enjoyed early success in the battle. But Athens was reluctant to send more than a token force. Had it been more aggressive it might have been able to help Argos defeat the Spartan army, which would have left Sparta isolated on the southern half of the peninsula, and without a large army to suppress a slave revolt. Fear of Spartan land power, however, prevented Athens from intervening in earnest.[25]

The return of tactical caution limited the prospects for strategic breakthrough. It also meant that bold commanders were hard to find. Most Athenians would not pursue campaigns that risked significant conflict with Sparta or Spartan allies on land. Even aggressive military leaders like Demosthenes sought to avoid open land battles.[26] Spartan commanders were much the same on the sea. As Thucydides noted, they were especially risk-averse when 'finding themselves involved in a maritime struggle, which their organization had never contemplated'.[27] And when exceptional commanders tried to buck this trend, they usually did so over the objections of civilian authorities. In 422, for example, Brasidas launched an audacious campaign into central Greece – in direct contravention of Spartan policy – which culminated in the Battle of Amphipolis. Consolidating that victory might have allowed Sparta to use central Greece as a launch pad to inspire rebellions in Athenian colonies. But there were good reasons why Spartan leaders did not support Brasidas's effort, including the fact that his strategy required reinforcements that could not arrive as long as Athens dominated the sea. Stubborn cross-domain asymmetries made it difficult to transform tactical victories into meaningful strategic results.[28]

Deterred from fighting outside their preferred domain, Athens and Sparta tried to win without challenging the other's strategic centre of gravity. They attempted arms racing, deception, stealth and roundabout operations designed to break the deadlock. They also hoped to find new allies who would be able or at least willing to challenge the enemy on its domain, but these attempts failed. Athens half-heartedly supported Argos but was unwilling to do so if that meant risking a substantial number of Athenian hoplites in battle. Sparta did not secure meaningful Persian support until the tail end of the war, and by that time it was so exhausted that its ultimate triumph over Athens was fleeting.[29]

The stalemate did not start to break down until Athens' Sicilian expedition, nearly two decades into the war. Sicily was a disaster for Athens, of course, but even that catastrophe did not end its naval dominance, and it was able to rapidly rebuild the fleet and score convincing victories at Cynocessma (412), Cyzicus (411) and Arginusae (406). Still, the loss at Sicily was the first clear sign that Athens could be beaten at sea, and Sparta and its allies started chipping away at the balance. Later, Sparta took advantage of Athens' financial troubles by luring Athenian rowers with promises of better pay. The experience of battle, along with efforts to buy more experienced crews, allowed Sparta to finally challenge Athens on the sea. The war ended for all practical purposes when Sparta defeated Athens' fleet at Aegospotami in 404.

Grand strategy requires a clear understanding of the sources of national security. Athens and Sparta lost sight of their durable advantages before the Peloponnesian War, and they became increasingly insecure. This had pernicious consequences for strategy after the fighting began. As described above, it caused them to grasp for strategic palliatives – military concepts that promised victory without having to confront their enemy directly. By the time these were revealed as delusions, the war was invested with huge political stakes. Worse yet, existential fears were overwhelming practical political objectives that might have served as useful strategic anchors. Both sides believed that they were fighting not just for their own survival, but for the future of the Greek world. The Spartan slogan 'Free the Greeks' conveyed the belief that Athens sought imperial dominion. The Athenians feared that Spartan treachery, epitomised by its habit of supporting factions and encouraging civil conflicts, foreshadowed an unstable and violent future. These beliefs hardened as the war expanded, blocking efforts to make the kind of peace that would have served everyone's strategic interest.

\*    \*    \*

US President George H.W. Bush was concerned about international turmoil at the end of the Cold War. Any triumphalism surrounding the demise of the Soviet Union was tempered by the fear that radical changes in the international system would open

the door for large-scale violence, as states suddenly sensed opportunities to settle old territorial disputes. For states bearing old
grudges, the dissolution of a great power might mean a chance to
right what they saw as historical wrongs. Other states might have
less of a historical claim; they simply seek to exploit international
instability for the purpose of predation. Bush himself stressed the
importance of respecting international borders and honouring
the pre-existing rights of sovereign states. This was, in fact, one of
the main arguments he made for going to war against Iraq after
its invasion of neighbouring Kuwait. Moments of international
change are also moments of great danger, and Bush wanted to
prevent a spiral of reciprocal score-settling and revanchism. He
also sought to protect Cold War international institutions as pillars
of stability in uncertain times. Ironically, the public champion of
the 'new world order' was mostly concerned with the status quo.

Bush's successors carried on with his approach. They celebrated
the basic tenets of what became known as the liberal international
order: democracy, trade and institutional cooperation. Despite
their differences across a range of policy issues, Democratic and
Republican administrations made these basic ideas the bedrock of
US grand strategy. They also believed that the US was indispensable; US military and economic power were vital to the health of the
order, which itself protected US security and prosperity. Exporting
US principles in the service of international order would make the
world safer while extending its own relative advantages.[30]

Cracks in bipartisan support for this grand strategy, however,
have grown over the last two decades. Frustration with the performance of international institutions dovetailed with suspicions
that allies were free-riding off US largesse. Strategic failures in the
wars in Iraq and Afghanistan, and the growing costs of maintaining a global military posture, fuelled questions about the wisdom
of the American approach. The rise of China and the 2008 financial crisis also damaged the assumption that US hegemony was

durable or desirable. Some argued that the US was turning away from an ideologically infused grand strategy based on the energetic promotion of US values. This shift was usually associated with President Donald Trump, an unapologetic nationalist who mocked international institutions and promised a ruthless and explicitly self-interested approach. But discontent about grand strategy was growing long before Trump's election. Indeed, it was part of the reason he won.[31]

Meanwhile, a sense of urgency has crept into China's grand strategy. Beijing has watched the US closely since the end of the Cold War, both because it was impressed by US capabilities and because it was constrained by US power. There were limits to what it could do about the status quo, however, given its economic struggles and military weakness. A quarter-century of economic and military growth changed its calculus, and US officials are concerned that China is now taking steps to reshape the international order. Not only is China becoming more aggressive in enforcing its regional maritime claims, but it is also seeking to inject illiberal norms into international institutions. All of this reflects an accelerated push for national rejuvenation and an ambitious effort towards a Sinocentric regional order. US officials fear that China has abandoned its prior approach, which sought to gain prosperity and guarantee the future of the Chinese Communist Party without provoking an international backlash. Those days are over; China's theory of security now requires confrontation.[32]

Not all observers agree about the trajectory of China's grand strategy. Some see more continuity in its approach, and they warn against overreaction. From their perspective, Beijing's aspirations are noteworthy but they are not fundamentally different from those of other great powers.[33] And because a lingering sense of material weakness motivates China's military activities, they warn against any US responses that increase Chinese insecurity. Doing so would inadvertently set off a downward spiral, making conflict more likely.[34] A less sanguine perspective is that Xi Jinping's particular definition of 'rejuvenation' does not allow for the kind of compromise that would alleviate a looming security dilemma. Moreover, China may perceive a brief window of opportunity to achieve its national goals before latent demographic and economic problems conspire against it. This combination of ambition and anxiety – not unlike what we saw in the ancient world – may encourage aggression.[35]

If the US and China are losing faith in their previous grand strategies, as was the case for Athens and Sparta, then trouble is coming. The same insecurity may cause leaders to fear that war is inevitable, and that in turn will increase the likelihood that they welcome strategic concepts that promise a quick and decisive victory. But like the ancient Greeks, modern strategists on both sides confront a daunting set of problems. China faces the most technologically sophisticated military power in history, one that can boast extraordinary capabilities in all domains. It also faces the dilemma about launching an amphibious operation against Taiwan, which would be the most likely cause of a war with the US. Such landings are inherently difficult. A Taiwan landing would be especially hard given the topology of the island and the small sliver of territory suitable for establishing a beachhead. China's most important attributes – its huge army and its territorial depth – would probably be irrelevant in such a campaign.[36]

The US also faces severe challenges. In the event of a conflict, it will need to mobilise forces from other theatres to fight in the Indo-Pacific; cobble together a joint effort across vast distances; ensure the integrity of communications in an era of cyber attacks and electronic warfare; and operate against a highly motivated and very lethal great-power rival operating in its maritime backyard. Fighting in this kind of 'contested zone' will be especially demanding given China's deliberate investment in sensors and weapons designed to attack incoming forces.[37]

Reducing the cost of fighting is vital for both countries given that a hypothetical future conflict would unfold under the shadow of nuclear weapons. It would be surprising to learn that the great powers were not searching for war-fighting options that took nuclear weapons out of play. But deliberate efforts to reduce the danger of escalation, for example by avoiding provocative strikes on the mainland, may inadvertently lead to a protracted war. The reason is that wartime caution would give the combatants an implicit refuge. In a situation in which both sides can safely retreat, neither has immediate incentives to seek terms. And if the perceived political stakes are very high, as would almost surely be the case in a US–China conflict, then a settlement involving mutual concessions will be unlikely.[38]

This scenario is not so different from the pattern of events before and during the Peloponnesian War. In that case, a crisis of confidence in pre-war grand strategy coincided with mutual recognition of each side's relative weaknesses. But recognition did not stop the march to war. Instead, it encouraged leaders to grab hold of strategic ideas that allowed them to fight on their own terms. These ideas failed the test of war, but by that time it proved impossible for Athens and Sparta to extricate themselves from the war. The current case also features two great powers who have become less sure of their grand-strategic principles, and who are both preparing for conflict. The US and China suffer comparative disadvantages on land and sea, respectively, and neither side is oblivious to the cross-domain balance. And like the ancients, both sides have invested in capabilities designed to work around them.

The analogy is imperfect, of course. The hub-and-spokes system of bilateral US alliances in Asia is nothing like the structure of the Delian League. It includes far fewer allies and partners in the region; Athens had more to worry about. In addition, the modern great powers have a much greater economic margin of error. More flexible financial systems and supply chains have sharply reduced the danger of sudden and extreme shortages. As Francis J. Gavin has recently argued, the fundamental dilemmas of contemporary international politics are 'problems of plenty'. Rather than a global struggle over finite land and resources, these problems have resulted from overabundance: cheap global communications, for instance, have led to a massive glut of misinformation.[39] The issues that occupied Sparta and Athens were categorically different.

Strategic theorists have also been paying more attention to the long-war problem. Unlike the Greeks, who planned for a short conflict, contemporary observers are theorising the pathways to protraction and debating the feasibility of sustaining operations over months or years.[40] Put another way, they are having the hard conversation that Athens and Sparta avoided. The unexpected war of attrition in Ukraine has pushed this debate forward. Russia clearly believed that it would win quickly – as did many Western observers. The fact that it did not, and that the conflict has become bogged down, has led to questions about the causes and conduct of protracted war. This is a welcome trend. Growing awareness of the danger of an exhausting conflict might inject some caution into US and Chinese diplomacy.

Or it might not. The forces driving great-power competition may overwhelm calls for caution based on careful analysis and long-term forecasting. This was the fate of Archidamus, whose prescient warnings were politely ignored. Ambitious great powers are also prone to blunders as they let enthusiasm for expansion get the better of prudent policy. Pericles warned the Athenians to guard against such errors, but he could not stop them.[41] Keeping strategy and grand strategy in alignment is particularly hard when rising great powers are simultaneously worried about their rivals. This strange blend of self-confidence and self-doubt plagued the ancient great powers. It returned in the modern era, as the next chapter shows, with unexpected consequences.

## CHAPTER TWO

# Britain and France in the American Revolution

Grand strategy explains why war is necessary. Strategy describes how to fight and win. If a state's theory of security is sound, then a coherent theory of victory will support long-term interests. But if the premises of grand strategy are flawed, then its relationship to strategy can become perverse. Wartime success can delude leaders into believing that their underlying theory of security is appropriate, obscuring all the reasons it is not. In these cases, excellent strategic choices will lead to wartime glory – and leave the state worse off. The converse is that strategic blunders are sometimes healthy in the long term because they force a reckoning about the real sources of state power. When states go to war in the service of a bad grand strategy, losing is the best thing that can happen.

French strategy in the American War of Independence was exceptional. What began as covert financial support to the American insurgents grew into a formal alliance in 1778. Despite the vast ideological distance between the monarchical French and

One section of this chapter originally appeared in Joshua Rovner, 'History Is Written by the Losers: Strategy and Grand Strategy in the Aftermath of War', *Journal of Strategic Studies* (Advance online publication, February 2024, https://www.tandfonline.com). We thank the publisher for permission to republish here.

the revolutionary Americans, their military partnership proved highly productive. Meanwhile, French diplomats cobbled together an effective coalition among states with very different interests and objectives. Keeping the coalition together forced the British Royal Navy to fight across vast distances rather than concentrate its efforts against the Americans, and this left British armies vulnerable to siege. A combined operation led to the encirclement and surrender of the British force at Yorktown in September 1781 and effectively ended the war against the American revolutionaries. The House of Commons voted to end support for offensive action in North America in February 1782 and the government dissolved one month later. British officials engaged in prolonged and public finger-pointing in a desperate effort to avoid blame and save their reputations. France exulted.[1]

Strategic success against the British, however, was a disaster for grand strategy. The impact on the Anglo-French military balance, and the broader continental balance of power, attenuated quickly. The impact on French politics was much more profound. Because the Americans fought from a position of military poverty, they relied on growing material support from abroad. As a result, France had to support a fledgling allied army across the Atlantic in addition to sustaining its own military and naval operations. All of this put enormous strain on French finances, at a time when it lacked the financial tools to accommodate a growing debt burden. It was not clear that the monarchy could realise its post-war international vision – or even that it could manage growing domestic unrest.

The British had the opposite experience. Britain's naval strategy in the war was plagued by indecision at key moments, and the various components of its army did not coordinate their actions effectively. British strategists operated under dubious assumptions about loyalist commitment in the colonies. They struggled to consolidate important battlefield victories, especially in the southern campaign, and they were never able to drive a wedge between the Americans and their vital foreign sponsors. Britain scored memorable tactical successes, both on sea and on land, but it could not translate them into strategic gains.

The shocking wartime defeat led to a vicious fight about who was responsible. Political and military leaders levied accusations against their rivals and scrambled to salvage their own reputations. But a more important debate was also under way, as officials reconsidered the value of what they had lost. Critics of the war had already argued that the cost of maintaining a large military presence in North America was prohibitive. In addition, the price of stability would rise as restive Americans grew increasingly frustrated with living under enforced colonial governance. Great Britain might have held on to the Thirteen Colonies, but the critics warned that doing so was counterproductive. Committing to the American project meant that other lucrative colonies might receive less attention. Hindsight suggests that a longer commitment to retaining the Thirteen Colonies would also have delayed the modernisation of the Royal Navy, the main instrument of imperial expansion. Losing the war elevated the critics' position, setting Great Britain on the path to a naval grand strategy that proved remarkably successful.

Comparing the French and British experiences is a good way of exploring the odd and sometimes counter-intuitive relationship between strategy and grand strategy. France conceived and executed a brilliant strategy, but suffered for its success in the long run. Great Britain's strategy was deeply flawed from the start, but its grand strategy benefited from the shock of losing.

## France's contradictory grand strategy

Prominent scholars have argued that revenge was the primary driver of French grand strategy before the war. French leaders 'husbanded their outrage and dreamed of revenge', declared Robert Middlekauff, after losing to Great Britain in the Seven Years' War (1756–63).[2] Samuel Flagg Bemis, widely regarded as the dean of diplomatic history in the first half of the twentieth century, wrote that French determination 'to undo the prostration of their country in 1763 by getting revenge on Great Britain as soon as the opportunity should present itself is the basic explanation of French foreign policy from 1763–1783'.[3] French grand strategy, however, was not simply an expression of resentment. By the time of the American revolt, it had evolved into a recognisable and defensible theory of security, inspired in part by its experience in the last war. Its approach was problematic, as we will see below, but it was much more than an expression of collective indignation against the British.

French grand strategy was built on three pillars. The first was the need for a more durable fiscal policy, which would put the administrative state on firmer ground while shoring up French industry. All of this would strengthen France's economic and war-fighting strength.

The French government already carried a substantial debt burden before the war, which frustrated early attempts to expand the navy. Indeed, France's desire to ally with Spain (ruled by another branch of the Bourbon dynasty) was an acknowledgement that it did not have the financial wherewithal to build the kind of navy that could threaten the British on its own.[4] France also lacked the kind of defence industry that could provide economies of scale. What it had instead was a scattered collection of uncoordinated firms. Its iron industry, for example, 'was collectively substantial but technically backward, scattered in small and often remote units'.

Efforts to cobble together supply chains were often improvised, inefficient and costly.[5] This precarious situation stood in the way of military modernisation.[6]

Louis XVI, who took the throne in 1774, was concerned about French finances. Notably, Louis appointed Anne-Robert-Jacques Turgot as Comptroller General.[7] Turgot sought not only to raise government revenue but also to bring order to France's confusing and inefficient tax system.[8] Doing so would inject some vitality into a sluggish French economy, and it might ultimately enable more thoroughgoing efforts to bolster French military power. But nothing like that would be possible until after major fiscal reforms took hold. Until then, France should exercise restraint and resist the urge to embark on risky diplomacy and costly military projects. Turgot opposed French involvement in the American war, and he pushed back against plans for a modest fleet expansion.[9]

The second pillar was geopolitical. French national security on the continent depended on maintaining the balance among great powers and minor states. France's alliance with the Habsburg dynasty helped to keep Austria and Prussia divided while simultaneously balancing against Russia. France also relied on a string of minor states, from the semi-autonomous Austrian Netherlands to the Republic of Genoa, which served as a buffer against possible threats from the east. This complex network of greater and lesser powers helped to protect French security, but it required careful attention.

And there were reasons to fear this network was coming apart. Foreign minister Charles Gravier, Comte de Vergennes, was particularly concerned about relations with Austria, which seemed increasingly volatile following the elevation of Joseph II to co-regent in 1765. If the Franco-Habsburg alliance broke down, France was at risk of isolation on the continent.[10] Meanwhile, the string of minor states would only serve as an effective buffer if France could reliably extend deterrence over them. French officials feared that the loss of prestige after the Seven Years' War would reduce the credibility of their promises – as well as the credibility of threats against possible aggressors. Ominously, great powers seemed increasingly interested in aggression and unconcerned with norms against territorial expansion at the expense of weaker powers. The recent 'despoiling of Poland' was especially alarming to France because it challenged the norm of sovereignty. As Vergennes put it, 'if force is right, if convenience is a title, what will henceforth be the security of states?'.[11]

The third pillar was the need to reduce the relative power gap with Great Britain. British economic might was a source of continuous concern to French leaders, especially given the dominance of the Royal Navy. Much as the Spartans had worried about the rise of Athenian naval power, French officials worried that if they did not close this power gap their British counterparts would not be able to resist the impulse to dominate. An overbearing naval power might coerce its rivals by controlling seaborne commerce and threatening to blockade friendly ports. In 1766, one contemporaneous observer conveyed the views of the French king to the British chargé d'affaires in Madrid: 'as Masters of the Sea, [the British were] too powerful not to be oppressive, and [he] is firmly of the opinion that no Peace with them can be secure'.[12]

At the same time, France was keen to avoid a serious confrontation, and Louis XVI was cautious about causing any kind of international trouble when he took the throne.[13] This posture was partly out of respect for British military power and concern about the outcome of another war. But it was also borne of a belief in some circles that long-term French security meant coming to terms with Great Britain. Reaching a durable modus vivendi with the dominant sea power in Europe would allow France to focus its defences on land, while simultaneously managing tenuous diplomatic relations with its continental allies and partners. Although Vergennes become associated with the American war later, in his tenure as foreign minister, he did not foresee a direct confrontation with Great Britain. Diplomacy, he believed, should work in the other direction. Vergennes idolised Cardinal Fleury, the powerful prime minister who had brought security to France by improving relations with Great Britain before his death in 1743.[14]

This position was not universally shared. Turgot's desire for fiscal reform and Vergennes's vision of detente were inconsistent with the lingering desire for revenge among powerful officials in Versailles. The desire to reduce British power was in tension with the desire to maintain diplomatic harmony. Efforts to satisfy these contradictory impulses were never going to succeed. And in any case, some French leaders cared less about amicable relations than about restoring national prestige after the humiliation of the Seven Years' War.[15] Perhaps the most prominent example was the Duc de Choiseul, the influential statesman and finance minister in the interwar period who sought to rebuild naval and military power 'for a war of revanche'.[16]

There was, of course, a deeper tension in Vergennes's approach. His desire to close the gap between French and British naval power risked embarrassing Great Britain, which took enormous pride in its Royal Navy. Why the British would have tolerated this kind of status reversal was not clear, though Vergennes seemed to believe that London would be more amenable to French interests if it was less sure of its naval mastery. This may look like wishful thinking in hindsight, but it was not an unreasonable belief at the time. Cardinal Fleury's early diplomatic success, after all, had come before Britain's naval triumph in the Seven Years' War and before it had launched an ambitious fleet-modernisation scheme.[17]

To summarise: French leaders wanted to restore state finances, reduce the relative power gap with Great Britain and shore up the balance of power in continental Europe. Each component of French grand strategy made sense on its own. These were reasonable aspirations for a great power looking for security at a moment of deep political instability. The problem, however, was that France's goals worked at cross purposes. Unwilling to make difficult trade-offs among competing priorities, the French implemented a contradictory grand strategy that worked against itself.

Efforts to reduce British power undermined the demand for fiscal prudence. Vergennes and others hoped that clandestine support for an American rebellion, as opposed to formal entry into a conventional war, would allow France to raise the cost to its rival without taking much from the French treasury. The problem, however, was that the Americans were fighting from a position of extreme military poverty. When hostilities began in earnest in 1775, they scrambled to assemble an army from a collection of part-time militias, and they had no real navy. Sustaining any kind of meaningful combat against a much larger enemy would inevitably require a large infusion of money and arms. And because such a small power could not be expected to win quickly, it would need additional resources as the fight went on. The desire to bleed the British by helping the Americans might prove irresistible, no matter the additional burden on French finances. The problem would only deepen if France felt compelled to provide direct assistance.

Astute French observers saw the risk. In his famous *Essai Général de Tactique* (1772), Jacques-Antoine-Hippolyte, Comte de Guibert offered a pessimistic analysis of contemporaneous conflict: 'We open our campaigns with armies that are neither adequately recruited nor properly paid. Whether they win or lose, both sides are equally exhausted. The National Debt increases, credit sinks, money runs out. Navies can find no more sailors, armies no more soldiers.' The danger was greater in France given its inflexible financial system; Britain could finance its debts over the long term. Guibert imagined a future in which states knew 'how to make war cheaply and to subsist on its victories', but that was not the case for France when he made his argument.[18]

Turgot shared these concerns and warned against supporting the Americans, which would ease the path to confrontation with Great Britain. Such a conflict was both expensive and unnecessary, given his belief that the Crown would not be able to control the Americans forever. Turgot assumed that the colonies would eventually break free of London, and that they would be eager to trade with France in the aftermath. But Turgot was unable to convince the king to hold the line, and he was increasingly isolated at court. Louis authorised one million livres-worth of munitions for the Americans on 2 May 1776. Turgot was forced to resign ten days later.[19]

Ironically, Vergennes agreed with Turgot that Great Britain would not be able to subdue the Americans forever. 'It will be in vain', he commented after the Battle of Bunker Hill in 1775, 'for the English to multiply their forces there … no longer can they bring that vast continent back to dependence by force of arms'.[20] But he could not resist the temptation to help the Americans bleed the British during their protracted exit. Watching the Crown throw good money after bad was especially satisfying as long as France remained officially neutral. But France's approach was already proving costly. Its naval spending alone had risen from 27.9m livres in 1774 to 42.6m in 1776, and that number was bound to rise as the French committed to supporting the Americans while guarding their

Caribbean possessions from the British fleet.[21] The desire to reduce British strength was already undermining the effort to stabilise the French budget.

Finally, the decision to fight Great Britain in North America potentially cut against France's need to attend to the European balance of power. French military attention was increasingly focused on North America, and naval activity in the Caribbean. Sustaining these operations required coordinating a multinational force and maintaining an elaborate logistics chain across the Atlantic. It also required difficult and continuing diplomacy with Spain and the Netherlands about the conduct of joint naval operations in the North Sea and the Mediterranean. Efforts to bolster continental allies, large and small, took a back seat to the exigencies of a distant war. That said, broad European antipathy to growing British naval power, as well as existing controversies among the eastern great powers, presented strategic opportunities that might allow France to sustain its buffer without direct military action.

## French strategy and the trouble with victory

France's limited intervention helped sustain the American insurgency in the first three years of the war, but at a growing cost. By the end of 1777, key advisers to Louis XVI had come to doubt the wisdom of their limited intervention, an approach that aimed to slowly ratchet up the costs to Great Britain without overstretching French resources. They were particularly concerned that the British would accept a negotiated peace after the Battle of Saratoga, putting their relations with the Americans on a more durable foundation and leaving France without any appreciable diplomatic gain. American envoys sensed an opportunity to exploit these concerns by urging the French to join the war directly, and to publicly proclaim that the goal was complete independence. Such a declaration would spoil British hopes that they could cut their military losses without paying a geopolitical price. The French agreed.

Overt support for American independence exposed the contradictions in pre-war French grand strategy. By fighting Great Britain directly, France was able to take a bite out of British military power. But the longer it fought, the more it compounded fiscal problems at home and festering diplomacy on the continent. France fought well, as we will see, but its hard-won strategic triumph was a long-run disaster.

France's wartime strategy was successful in many ways. Firstly, French naval and military movements overstretched British forces, preventing them from concentrating against the vulnerable American army. Absent the French intervention, the Royal Navy might have patrolled the coastline and rivers to partition the North American theatre, effectively creating 'islands' on land. Doing so would have complicated American communications, squeezed their economy and made it much harder to find refuge in the face of British army offensives. France's treaty with the Americans made this impossible, compelling the Royal Navy to spread its forces across the Caribbean, the English Channel, the Mediterranean Sea and India. Worse yet, from London's perspective, it increased the difficulty of resupplying any British army campaigns away from major cities under British control.[22]

France's navy was a threat-in-being to the British. The presence of 60 uncrewed ships at Brest, Toulon and Rochefort forced London to pay attention. The later addition of 50 Spanish ships gave Bourbon naval forces the ability to harass the Royal Navy in the English Channel and simultaneously threaten its position in the Mediterranean.[23] None of this would be possible, however, if the fleet remained at port, because this would put the combined fleet at risk of blockade or defeat in detail. In any case, neither France nor Spain wanted to stay put.

The French needed to protect their possessions in the Caribbean and the Spanish needed to protect lucrative convoys returning from its colonies. Both countries also sought to put British possessions at risk. Spain wanted to seize Minorca, West Florida and Gibraltar. France wanted, at a minimum, to use seized land as bargaining chips. None of this would be possible if the fleets stayed at home.[24]

The decision to challenge the Royal Navy was certainly daring, given France's dubious track record in previous wars. Effective French naval strategy required more than boldness, given the range of possibilities in the coming conflict: maritime support for the Americans, offensive and defensive fleet actions to improve the French position in the Caribbean, an intensifying contest for dominance in India, efforts to wrest Gibraltar and Minorca from British control, and a possible operation against Great Britain itself. Allocating resources to different theatres would require a careful balance of aggression and restraint.[25]

In North America, for example, the French priority was less the destruction of British warships and more the maintenance of reliable communications with the Continental Army and, after 1780, the French expeditionary force. Glorious victories in fleet-on-fleet engagements were not required for this task. In some cases, an indecisive draw might be enough. However tactically unsatisfying, it made a great deal of strategic sense, and France's maritime approach was appropriately geared towards supporting land operations.[26] Whereas the Royal Navy used powerful short-range cannon to fire at enemy hulls, French warships targeted British sails and masts. The point was not to sink Royal Navy vessels or kill in large numbers, which would entail serious risks for French warships, but to hamper British naval operations. Doing so provided relief for American and French forces on land, who worried about being cut off from seaborne supplies.[27]

Secondly, France conducted highly effective joint operations with the Continental Army in North America. Successful coordination was far from inevitable and French officials deserve credit for managing what might otherwise have been a very fraught relationship. The two countries, after all, had profound religious and ideological differences, and deep prejudices coloured their relations.[28] Some Americans were concerned that asking for French military assistance might inadvertently lead to French political control, and they debated internally about whether a future alliance should be restricted to commercial exchange. They also reasonably wondered if France would commit to fighting all the way to independence, given the costs.[29]

France partially alleviated these concerns by making independence an explicit goal in the Treaty of Alliance in 1778, though the alliance was on rocky ground from the start. The first major land–sea collaboration, in fact, was a debacle. A Continental Army under Major General John Sullivan was attempting to eject the British from Newport, Rhode Island, a deep-water harbour accessible through a relatively narrow channel into Narragansett Bay. By virtue of its geography, Newport was defensible and an appealing base of operations for the incoming French squadron led by Admiral d'Estaing, which included 12 ships of the line and delivered 4,000 troops for American duty. The operation started well: the British knew that they could not prevent the French from sailing through the channel, so they sank several of their own vessels to complicate navigation. Soon, however, a smaller Royal Navy squadron arrived and began to patrol just outside the entrance to the bay. D'Estaing sailed out to meet the enemy, setting the stage for what one scholar calls 'the most interesting fleet battle in the age of sail that was never fought'.[30] As the opposing sides were manoeuvring for advantage in advance of their expected confrontation, an unusually severe storm blew in across the Rhode Island coast, throwing both sides into disarray and badly damaging several French ships. D'Estaing broke off the battle and took his limping squadron to Boston for repairs. The Continentals who were waiting outside Newport were furious at being abandoned, and the French were met with hostility when they arrived in Boston. Anger over the battle that never was mingled with old bigotries, leading some observers to fear for the future of the nascent alliance. Continental leaders, including George Washington himself, acted quickly to undo the harm.[31]

The quality of coalition operations improved as the war went on. Although the French failed to bring the Royal Navy to decisive action in 1778–79, their tactics improved, along with their working relations with the Continental Army and Congress.[32] When the French expeditionary army landed in 1780, French military officers did not try to dominate operational planning. Their restraint is noteworthy given the Americans' desperate need for French support; it would not have been surprising to see French officers treat the Continental Army as something like a client state. But they largely resisted the temptation to seize wartime control. The king authorised the Comte de Rochambeau to lead the French force but ordered him to accept a subordinate position to Washington. Rochambeau made no effort to undermine the order, or take control indirectly, despite having many more years of military experience than his American counterpart. By allowing Washington to lead, he deferred to local knowledge and hard-won experience. He also pre-empted any concerns about coalition disunity and enabled the culminating victory at Yorktown.[33]

The Yorktown campaign itself was a model of strategic flexibility. Washington and Rochambeau had planned operations around New York in May 1781 to compel General Henry Clinton to recall troops from Virginia and relieve pressure on American forces in the south. Rochambeau had urged Washington to consider marching south instead, sensing an opportunity to defeat the British force under General Charles Cornwallis. As late as 19 July Washington still believed that New York should be the coalition's primary target, but intelligence that Cornwallis was heading east suggested an opportunity to trap him against the Virginia coast. Rochambeau's view prevailed, and Washington began preparing to turn the army southward. This included coordinating with Admiral François Joseph Paul de Grasse, who would sail his fleet up the coast to block the Royal Navy from reinforcing Cornwallis, as well as an elaborate deception operation to convince British army leaders that New York remained the allies' destination.[34]

The march south was impressive. A combined army totalling over 7,000 moved southwest through Philadelphia towards the head of the Elk River, where forces would sail down the Chesapeake Bay before coming back north and landing at Jamestown, to the west of Cornwallis. Not enough boats were ready, however, so many forces marched to Baltimore and Annapolis to secure alternative transport.

By this time de Grasse had already arrived outside Yorktown, where he delivered marines to General Lafayette to support his ongoing harassment of Cornwallis. De Grasse could have simply parked his squadron in the entrance to the York River to prevent the Royal Navy from reaching Cornwallis, but doing so would have put a separate French fleet at risk: Admiral Barras was simultaneously sailing from Newport with siege guns and other equipment needed for the final effort against the beleaguered British force, and the Royal Navy was coming as well. Instead of remaining in the bay, de Grasse sailed out to meet the British ships. The following Battle of the Virginia Capes was indecisive tactically, but hugely important strategically. Barras got through; the Royal Navy did not.

At this point the end seemed almost a foregone conclusion, but siege operations are complex, requiring a combination of engineering, fortitude and grim arithmetic. Rochambeau, a veteran of siege warfare, understood the dangers of going too fast (and putting the advancing army in danger) as well as going too slow (which would depress morale and increase the chance that some unexpected event, like a change in the weather, might work against the blockading naval force). He urged Washington to adopt a methodical middle ground, slowly but persistently squeezing the circle around Yorktown and reducing the range necessary for accurate cannon fire. This approach succeeded. Cornwallis surrendered on 19 October 1781.

Thirdly, France deftly managed its broader wartime coalition. Indeed, this was one of the more impressive aspects of French strategy during the war. Diverting British military and naval force away from North America meant crafting operations that would pose real dangers to British interests elsewhere. France needed powerful allies that could bolster its own forces in multiple regions. Gaining their cooperation, however, required delicate and often frustrating diplomacy, mixing accommodations and exhortations in order to satisfy partners with very different political goals.

Spain was especially important, given the size of its navy. A combined French and Spanish fleet would exceed the Royal Navy in ships and guns, making it possible to open new theatres of operation.[35] Access to Spanish ports would allow the alliance to pose a continuous threat to Gibraltar and Minorca, the cornerstones of Britain's position in the Mediterranean. Moreover, a combined armada could plausibly threaten the English Channel, though there were considerable dangers in any such campaign.

Spain was a hard sell, however, and convincing it to join the war would take years of persistent diplomatic effort. It was still not ready even after the American victory in the Battle of Saratoga in 1777, which provided France a pretext for a formal alliance. Despite its dream of reclaiming Gibraltar, Spain was wary of taking on the Royal Navy on behalf of a distant republican revolution, and it preferred to keep its distance from the expanding war. France's decision to break off relations with Great Britain, however, was a diplomatic fait accompli, because it made it risky for Spain to remain neutral.[36]

Vergennes finally secured Spanish support through the Treaty of Aranjuez in April 1779. The difficulty in convincing Spain to join the war was then replaced by the challenge of sustaining the partnership. This included a blend of persuasion and accommodation, as Spanish objectives grew during the war. The allies concocted an ill-fated joint campaign to occupy the Isle of Wight and then the mainland itself at Portsmouth, all with an eye towards gaining leverage over London so that it would return Gibraltar to Spain. The logistics alone made the idea dubious: the campaign would require 40,000 troops and 8,000 cavalry mounts and place an additional burden on French shipping. Vergennes soured on the operation and tried to nudge Spain away from it, but he went along with the plan in order to keep the Spanish on board. As it happened, the 1779 armada petered out. A combination of disease, foul weather and bureaucratic confusion conspired against the campaign. However embarrassing at the time, the strategic result was probably for the best. France could claim that it had supported its ally but that its plans had failed for reasons beyond anyone's control. French diplomats also placated Spain by promising to help protect its western approaches, all the while discouraging Spanish entreaties for another try at the English coast.[37]

The alliance found more success later. Bernardo de Gálvez, acting governor of Spanish-controlled Louisiana, could have requested the use of a portion of de Grasse's fleet before it sailed for Yorktown in 1781, but he did not. Releasing the whole fleet improved the odds of blocking the British effort to resupply Cornwallis's beleaguered force in Virginia. French–Spanish coordination flourished in other ways. Francisco de Saavedra served as de Grasse's principal aide, and together they drew up plans for the Yorktown campaign. This happy partnership was not simply the product of personal trust between de Grasse and de Saavedra. It was, instead, the culmination of several years of diligent coalition diplomacy.[38]

In addition to maintaining relations with Spain, Vergennes finalised a treaty with Holland, 'so long a virtual British client state'.[39] Although the Dutch did not have the same firepower as the other combatants in the war, the alliance helped ease the French supply problem. France relied on timber from Prussia and the Baltic states and had applied economic pressure on the Dutch to escort transport ships from these areas – despite intense British protests. Formalising the agreement helped relieve French anxiety about naval stockpiles of masts, hemp and timber, a problem that predated the American conflict. Importantly, it also gave Britain another enemy to worry about. Nimble coalition diplomacy paid off.[40]

Fourthly, French officials had a very good sense of timing. Fools rush into war, but the French did not. Instead, they began with a cautious and clandestine outreach effort in 1774, quietly sounding out American revolutionaries to gauge their intentions and capabilities. This led, the next year, to a covert effort to fund the insurgency, using a false corporate entity as cover for French assistance.[41] British officials soon learned of the covert assistance, to their dismay, but they did not view it as a *casus belli*. So France was able to sustain its proxies without provoking direct confrontation with its great-power rival.[42] This suggested an optimal path for French wartime diplomacy: supporting the Americans indirectly and covertly might help wear down British power without putting French forces at risk. And if nothing else, it provided an opportunity to collect information on North America that might prove vital in the event that France intervened directly.

France continued to provide limited support during 1776–77, a strategy designed to impose costs on the British by extending the war without direct French involvement. Sustaining the fiction of French neutrality proved increasingly difficult, given signs that Paris was allowing American privateers to operate from French ports. It was also difficult because American envoys were increasingly desperate for a formal and overt French alliance. From their perspective, limited intervention would never be enough to overcome British power in North America. What it did, however, was buy time to continue the French naval build-up and to cultivate support from Spain.[43]

Why did France make the decision to formally ally with the Americans? Some argue that it panicked after the Battle of Saratoga, fearing that the British would be willing to cut their losses and end the war.[44] French leaders were certainly concerned about a premature peace because they wanted to drive up British costs in a prolonged war. Yet there were signs that some French leaders already believed that they had extinguished the benefits from limited and unofficial participation. From their perspective, the battle was a pretext for joining the war in earnest, not a cause.[45] France also had a compelling reason to join the fight in 1778, when it could boast naval parity with Great Britain. French intelligence, however, suggested that the balance would shift in Britain's favour as it accelerated its naval mobilisation. Armed with these ominous forecasts, Vergennes became convinced that the time to act had arrived.[46]

France's timing compounded British problems. Great Britain's failure to destroy the Continental Army during the Hudson campaign caused it to retreat to cities, which it thought to use as bases for raids against American units in a war of attrition. The problem with this plan was that the army could not provide sufficient forces to cover the vast distances required in North America – especially after France entered the war and pulled British attention elsewhere. The need to maintain control of key colonies in the Caribbean, and to retain a strategic reserve in case of a real threat of an invasion via the English Channel, limited the number of troops that London could safely deploy. Vergennes exploited the situation by sending a naval squadron to protect French assets and contest the Royal Navy in the Western Hemisphere, while maintaining bases in northern France to unsettle the British. He hoped that Britain was so overstretched that the French navy could achieve a decisive victory without the Spanish, whose participation was far from assured.[47]

Not everything went according to plan. The French fleet under d'Estaing was unable to bring the British to a fleet-on-fleet engagement off the North American coast. It finally engaged the Royal Navy off St Lucia in December, but it withdrew after two unsuccessful assaults against the British line. And while the British were holding the line in the Caribbean, they were gaining ground elsewhere. France's opening campaign in India was a disaster: all of its posts there would fall by 1779.[48] Despite the fact that the French navy had overstretched British forces, it was becoming clear that it could not prevail unless it was able to secure Spain's entry.

Vergennes's political and diplomatic effort went into overdrive. Convinced that expanding the alliance against Great Britain was vital for France's prospects in the war, he sent a personal letter to the king in December 1778 urging flexibility in meeting Spanish demands to entice their participation. Worried that France risked naval and financial ruin if it could not secure Spanish assistance, Vergennes warned Louis that 'his Majesty cannot struggle long on equal terms with the English'.[49]

France intervened in earnest in 1780, when it sent an expeditionary force to North America. This force would prove vital to the combined campaign that led to Cornwallis's surrender at Yorktown. Adding thousands of French troops to the Continental Army made the coalition force a threat-in-being to the British headquarters in New York. British commanders had to take seriously the danger of a joint offensive against the city, a fact that made it possible for Washington to deceive them into staying put as the Americans and French turned their attention to Virginia. The French also provided critical resources. The fleet under Admiral Barras that had sailed south from Newport, for example, delivered the siege train used at Yorktown.[50] Having provided essential reinforcements, French leaders encouraged bolder action, knowing that time for a decisive victory was running short. Officers in the French expeditionary force suspected that reinforcements were not coming soon, given rising tensions in Europe.[51]

France's wartime leaders knew when to make peace. Although the war on American land effectively ended after the autumn of 1781, intense naval action continued in the Caribbean. The naval fight was important to France, which was desperate to recover territories lost to the Royal Navy during the war thus far. Yet the balance of naval forces increasingly favoured the British, who were finally free to concentrate their capabilities against the French navy, and the costs to France were rising at an alarming rate. In April 1782, the dramatic Royal Navy victory at the Battle of the Saintes dashed any French hopes that the war had weakened British sea power. Instead, as naval historian John Reeve concludes, the battle 'revived British naval prestige to a significant political effect.

The perception in London and Paris was that the naval balance of power had been restored to that of the early 1760s: a perception that would greatly influence the peace treaties.'[52] The outcome surely helped disabuse French leaders of victory fever following the extraordinary British surrender at Yorktown. They knew it was time to end the war, and they worked as hard to convince their allies to stop fighting as they had worked to get them on board in the first place.

France executed a fine wartime strategy in the service of American independence. It forced Great Britain to disperse its forces from North America, alleviating the problem of the Continental Army's material weakness. It designed and implemented highly effective joint operations with the Americans. It worked hard to bring other states into the coalition and keep them actively engaged against British forces. And French strategists had a keen sense of when to intervene, when to escalate and when to stop fighting.

France's strategic success, however, did not make it safer. In fact, its extraordinary wartime triumph undermined the institutional foundations of French national security. Recall that France's grand strategy was animated by three goals: undermining British power, shoring up the continental balance and restoring French finances. In different ways, the American War of Independence worked against each of these objectives.

The war did little to undermine Britain's relative power advantages, especially after London proved in the aftermath that it could continue trading profitably with its erstwhile colonies. British exports to the colonies were about 90% of the pre-war average in the years immediately following the war, and by the 1790s they *exceeded* pre-war levels. Worse yet, from France's perspective, is that increasing demand for British exports led to rising British shipbuilding. The Royal Navy grew alongside commercial shipping, as did the relative gap between it and France. The gap would grow over time, putting French sea power at a grave disadvantage in coming conflicts.[53]

France's wartime strategy mostly worked against its grand strategy. The major exception was its effort to bolster the continental balance. Here French leaders deserve a great deal of credit, as they simultaneously played on the continental great powers' concerns about growing British naval power and their suspicions of one another. Vergennes sensed that disgruntlement over the Royal Navy's dominant maritime position, especially among Russia and Sweden, created an opportunity to choreograph a united front against it.[54] Rather than inviting the European powers into the war directly, he encouraged the creation of a League of Armed Neutrality, which eventually included Russia, Denmark, Sweden, Prussia, Austria and the Ottoman Empire. Focusing their attention on British sea power helped reduce the chance that they would act opportunistically against French allies on land.[55] At the same time, France took steps to end the war on terms that kept the European great powers from aligning too closely. As one historian puts it, the Treaty of Paris was critical for 'restraining the appetites of Prussia and the Hapsburg house of Austria, (and) playing off the Ottoman Empire against the steadily mounting pressure of Russia and also the United Provinces against the Hapsburgs'.[56] Restoring the great-power balance helped preserve the sovereignty of the buffer states along France's eastern frontier.

These gains were real, to be sure, but they came at a staggering cost. Indeed, France's success at maintaining its land buffer was far less meaningful than the long-term effects on the Anglo-French balance and the financial price tag. Not only did France incur enormous debt during the war, it also lacked the financial instruments to accommodate its growing burden. The decision for war had amounted to a rejection of Turgot's effort to restore French finances, and the conduct of the war compounded the problem. What had begun as a covert effort to sustain the American cause became an overt war against a global great power, requiring continuous naval operations in multiple theatres, a substantial expeditionary force in North America and financial support to the insurgents. Its calculated decision to escalate, a sensible choice in terms of strategy, was disastrous in terms of grand strategy. France nearly quadrupled its annual spending during the war. According to a close accounting of French finances, 'the cost to the French monarchy of aiding America to her independence is in excess of a billion livres'. And the problem did not stop at the war's end. The amount it paid to service the national debt from 1784–86 (181m livres) vastly exceeded its regular appropriations (106m livres).[57] While the war was not the only cause of the French financial crisis of 1786, it is inconceivable that the crisis would have occurred without it.[58]

France made a series of strategic decisions that made sense in terms of helping the Americans win their war. Each step was sensible in terms of French strategy. The cumulative effect, however, was to undermine French grand strategy. Vergennes was a capable diplomat with a keen understanding of coalition warfare. Yet he failed to grasp the underlying socio-economic problems in his own country that placed the monarchy on such precarious ground.[59] The departure of Turgot in 1776 removed the critical check on French profligacy, allowing French administrators to pour more resources into the effort. As a result, the financial demands of strategy prevailed over the financial restraint that French grand strategy badly needed.

The story of French finances is a vivid illustration of a deeper conceptual problem: crafting strategy in the service of a contradictory grand strategy. France's theory of security was based on objectives that worked at cross purposes. French officials wanted to reduce British power without damaging British relations, and they wanted to strengthen French finances while investing in a long war against a great-power enemy. These contradictions made French strategy an absurdity. By choosing to support the Americans – and then doubling down on that choice – the French monarchy jeopardised its own future. Victory obscured the damage to long-term national security.

## British grand strategy and the question of empire

If French grand strategy was plagued by contradictions, British grand strategy before the war was in flux. Starting in the early eighteenth century, Great Britain began the slow process of building the financial, administrative and naval infrastructure that it would exploit during the high-water mark of the Pax Britannica. But those imperial foundations were far from complete at the outset of the American revolution, and Britain's war to hold on to its colonies delayed the process. The shock of losing was necessary to start it again.[60]

British uncertainty was noteworthy, given that its grand strategy in the first half of the eighteenth century had been straightforward. The Crown sought land powers on the continent to balance French power, and a network of colonial outposts to generate resources and revenue. It asked a great deal of its continental allies but, at least before the Seven Years' War (1756–63), relatively little of its North American colonies, which enjoyed substantial political autonomy. What was most important was what the colonies *could not* do: go to war with each other; enforce regulations that contradicted British laws; or otherwise harm British economic interests.[61] Granting local autonomy made sense because it avoided stoking the colonists' Puritan independence streak, and because the British army had additional policing and war-fighting responsibilities elsewhere.[62]

The institutional basis of Britain's grand strategy, however, was incomplete. The boundaries of the administrative state were still being determined, and army reforms were very much a work in progress. Most important of all, British officials were still struggling to build the complex infrastructure underlying the Royal Navy. Shipbuilding was accelerating quickly, but Britain did not have the dockyards to handle maintenance for such a fast-growing fleet.[63]

The fleet itself was quite vulnerable. Because previous generations were built at about the same time, the emergence of hitherto hidden design flaws or material shortcomings could have sudden and disastrous effects. Overcoming this problem required a complex set of changes to the timing of shipbuilding, along with changes to materials storage, labour practices and dockyard management. Such mundane matters, however important to British grand strategy, were of little interest to most parliamentarians. Capturing their interest and winning new funding was difficult.[64] The First Lord of the Admiralty, the Earl of Sandwich, sought to put the Royal Navy on a firmer foundation in the 1760s through a series of naval reforms. These changes required substantial investment and careful negotiations with the dockyard officials and workers, who jealously guarded their own preferences.[65] The Royal Navy meanwhile continued its bureaucratic rationalisation, including frustratingly slow efforts to routinise the budget process.[66]

Victory in the Seven Years' War injected new urgency into naval modernisation. The thrill of victory mingled with new concerns about holding on to an expanding empire. In some ways, holding its new territories was more demanding than taking them, especially given the debt Britain incurred in the war and the fragility of its boom-and-bust economy. The American war, however, put reforms on hold. The Admiralty couldn't risk upsetting the naval industry while mobilising the fleet in 1775, or after the fighting began in earnest.[67]

Other elements of Sandwich's programme would have to wait until the war ended. Trouble in America also increased British economic uncertainty, giving some parliamentarians reasons to question naval investments. Financial volatility, highlighted by the spectacular crash of 1772, raised questions about whether the country could afford the costs of imperial expansion.[68]

The rapid growth of British colonies introduced practical questions about grand strategy. British leaders disagreed about how many forces were required to garrison the empire, and the extent to which they should operate inland from coastal enclaves.[69] They also disagreed on the value of America itself. Advocates of British rule made economic and political claims. They argued that high-quality timber from New England was vital for shipbuilding; that northern fisheries were needed to feed slave labourers in the Caribbean sugar plantations; and that port access along the American coast was essential for the Atlantic trade.[70] Others, including the king, warned that giving up the Thirteen Colonies would inspire others to rebel, and perhaps encourage other great powers to attack British interests. The king was particularly concerned about the ideological nature of the revolution, which suggested an end of the old monarchical order in Europe.[71]

Sceptics replied that maintaining control over all of North America was not vital to the empire. The truly lucrative colonies were in the West Indies and in India. Supplies of timber and fish, along with port access, were negotiable, especially because the colonists had huge economic incentives to work with Britain. Moreover, the peculiarities of the North American colonies suggested that others were not likely to follow their lead. The Americans, as Edmund Burke famously argued, were animated by a litigious brand of Protestantism not found elsewhere. These characteristics made it unlikely Britain would win quickly in the event of war, and certainly not decisively. Despite its vast material advantages at the outset of the war, critics warned that the political gulf was unsustainable, and that a war could at best provide a temporary respite from revolutionary activism.[72]

Some believed Britain stood a better chance in a notional 'war of interest' against France than a 'war of passion' against the Americans.[73] British grand strategy, in this formulation, rested on attacking France when and where it was exposed, rather than sinking resources into an unwinnable counter-insurgency in North America. These critics advocated a return to the loose style of imperial control that had served the country well when employed in North America in the first half of the century. History proved them correct. The expensive and futile effort to hold the Thirteen Colonies against their will represented a dangerous aberration in a period of political turmoil and economic uncertainty, and before the government had completed the institutional reforms needed to rationalise the bureaucracy and professionalise the navy.

### British strategy and the value of defeat

Grand-strategic uncertainty had major strategic consequences during the war. Firstly, British leaders could not agree on the definition of victory. There was no consensus about whether the goal was reconciliation or subjugation, and in the early years they tried to achieve both. While British forces tried to smash the Continental Army and cut off New England from the rest of the colonies, peace commissioners repeatedly made overtures to end the fighting and return to something like the status quo ante.[74] These efforts were self-defeating: Americans were suspicious about British intentions given the ferocity of the war, but the peace feelers gave them reason to doubt Great Britain's will to persist.

Secondly, it led to hedging strategies among leaders who disagreed about appropriate goals. King George III was determined to prosecute the war and force the Americans to give up their revolutionary aspirations, but Parliament was less enthusiastic. The prime minister, Lord Frederick North, was crucial to the Crown because there were few others who supported the war while also enjoying majority support. North was ambivalent, partly because he feared that it would lead to a conflict with France under unfavourable circumstances, and partly because he suspected the financial costs would outweigh the political benefit. Privately he urged the king to reconsider his position, and he repeatedly asked the king's permission to resign.

Britain's period of grand-strategic uncertainty ultimately deepened fissures among military and political leaders, who went to war with their own beliefs about the best course of action. George III treated the war as a test of willpower. North agreed for a time, but then reversed course and hoped that carrots rather than sticks would encourage the Americans to reconcile with the Crown.[75] After France's entry, the cabinet could not agree on whether to focus on the land war in North America or on naval operations in Europe. Lord George Germain, secretary of state for the American colonies, wanted to continue on land. Sandwich, however, argued that the greater risk to British national security was French naval superiority in European waters. The debate spilled into parliamentary arguments in spring 1778.[76]

The unresolved dispute among ministers ceded the initiative to French and American forces. As long as the government could not decide how to prioritise its objectives, it risked being overstretched on both sea and land. The navy struggled to protect and resupply the army, a problem that would continue up to Yorktown. Worse, the expansion of the war meant that it also struggled to keep up with French (and later Spanish) fleet movements. The percentage of British warships and troops deployed to North America declined precipitously after 1778, as they had to prepare for possible confrontations in other parts of the empire.[77]

Frustrated by the lack of clear and consistent guidance from London, military commanders feuded among themselves, sometimes fighting independently rather than coordinating their efforts. The disastrous Saratoga campaign in 1777 witnessed the failure to execute a plan to join armies marching from the north and south, which would have cut the colonies in half. The British loss stemmed from its failure to locate the strategic centre of gravity. Was it the network of North American waterways? Was it revolutionary fever in New England? Was it the Continental Congress? Or was it Washington's army? No one could answer affirmatively, so commanders decided for themselves, with terrible consequences. A similar dispute divided generals Clinton and Cornwallis during the southern campaign (1778–81). Clinton advocated a defensive strategy to consolidate British strongholds in South Carolina and slowly expand Loyalist support. Cornwallis argued for going on the offensive, on the logic that destroying the Americans' conventional forces was the only way to end the war decisively. The outcome *was* decisive, of course, but not in the way he intended.

British strategy was a dismal failure. Political and military leaders never settled on ends, or means, or how to connect them. The immediate result was internecine squabbling and public efforts to deflect blame. Over the long term, however, the war was a powerful reminder of the danger of costly land campaigns. Losing the war allowed the naval-reform effort to resume, and the Royal Navy restored its political position. Meanwhile, some in Parliament came to view the British army with suspicion, seeing it as the extension of the landed gentry, while others saw an opportunity to concentrate its training and deployment cycles. But the main result was to give more money and attention to the service most responsible for sustaining Britain's grand strategy. In the first two years after the war, about 40% of the entire national budget went to rebuilding the Royal Navy. A new comptroller set about rationalising the personnel system in the Admiralty. Commanders became more professional, communications improved at sea, and new techniques made naval gunfire more flexible and accurate. In sum, political attention in the wake of failure led to a strong and sustainable navy, capable of implementing an ambitious grand strategy and, if necessary, fighting well.[78]

These reforms slowly helped move Great Britain away from mercantilism towards a more productive economic regime. This transformation was not simply the triumph of private industry and visionary politicians. The Royal Navy, instead, served as a shield for the emergence of domestic innovation and a shift towards liberal trade. Naval modernisation did not guarantee that trade would be free, but it enabled commercial change. The economic historian Patrick K. O'Brien emphasises 'the benign loops' linking the navy with commercial, banking and shipbuilding interests that developed in the decades following the war. These links placed the Royal Navy 'at the hub of an evolving, integrating and progressive maritime sector of an Island economy'.[79]

Equally important, the American experience proved the sceptics right. Despite pre-war fears of falling dominoes, the empire did not collapse after the Americans won their independence. It became stronger. Unlike France, Britain managed its debts well during the fight and came out solvent, and its financial system continued to mature. Institutional reform and economic growth enabled Britain's grand strategy over the next century, and the memory of military disaster helped. It reinforced the old lesson that colonies mattered only insofar as they supported trade and the navy. As the historian N.A.M. Rodger neatly puts it, 'only in the atypical years of the mid-century did the British become obsessed with colonies for their own sake, and the debacle of the American War cured them of that'.[80] Strategic disaster paved the way for grand-strategic success.

*   *   *

France and Britain both entered the American war with flawed grand strategies. France's was contradictory, a collection of incompatible ideas about power, wealth and diplomacy. Some of these ideas were plausible in isolation, but they made little sense as part of a broader package. Strong and resilient states can live with such contradictions because they have room for error. France did not. The *ancien régime* was increasingly sagging under the weight of its antiquated financial system and rigid political and class structure. It could not easily afford the domestic or political consequences of a long war across the ocean. Any hopes of aligning strategy with grand strategy rested on fighting in such a way as to maximise efficiency and minimise costs. French leaders thought that a protracted conflict would erode British power, but the real effect was to expose the inherent problems at home.

Britain's grand strategy was uncertain and ultimately misguided. Victory over France in the Seven Years' War led to a massive expansion in British colonial possessions, but British officials could not agree on whether and how to keep them. Paradoxically, Britain's expansion made the Crown more sensitive to minor changes in the global balance, and more fearful of losing control.[81] Yet others, including distinguished parliamentarians, were sympathetic to the American cause, and they warned that throwing resources at the status quo was deeply misguided. These debates played out against the fraught backdrop of 1770s London, where global aspirations confronted economic and political apprehensions. Few could agree on the value of the American territories, either as colonies or as independent trading partners.

In France, pro-war advisers manoeuvred their critics out of positions of influence, and gradually brought the king on board. This allowed France to design and execute a coherent and effective strategy. It assembled an impressive coalition, forcing Great Britain to overstretch its forces, and worked well with the upstart Americans, combining sea and land power to great effect. In Great Britain, by contrast, persistent internal fissures led to half-hearted and inconsistent strategic decisions. In 1776 it enjoyed an overwhelming military advantage and a monopoly on real naval power over the Thirteen Colonies. Yet it was not able to capitalise on these material advantages, and its wartime blunders contributed to a strategic disaster.

The effects on grand strategy were the reverse. France suffered for its victory, and Britain gained from its defeat. France's wartime triumph did not reduce its relative disadvantage to Great Britain, which quickly set about restoring its naval lead. Nor did it put diplomatic relations with London on a more reliable course, as Vergennes hoped. Most important, of course, was the economic strain of the war on the French budget. The decision to support the Americans deepened its debt crisis and played a key role in its subsequent economic and political breakdown. The grand-strategic outcome was much better for Britain, not least because the war settled the debate about whether the empire could withstand the loss of its American colonies. In this way the war helped nudge Britain away from its mercantilist past. It also encouraged British leaders to refocus on naval modernisation, and to build the infrastructure of a naval trading empire.

The British experience foreshadowed that of the United States during the Cold War. Like their British forebears, US officials wrestled with the value of distant territories, and their debates were never really resolved. They also wrestled with questions of economic resiliency and protracted great-power competition. But twentieth-century technology complicated the relationship between strategy and grand strategy. In one sense, as we will see in the next chapter, it transformed an enduring problem into an existential dilemma.

## CHAPTER THREE

# Strategy and grand strategy in the Cold War

Uncertain grand strategies in peace increase the risk of erratic strategies in war. States that cannot settle on a reasonably well-defined theory of victory are likely to struggle to translate their latent military capabilities into lasting political results. One reason, as the British learned to their dismay in the American War of Independence, is that differing views about the real sources of national security have pernicious effects on civil–military relations. Competing grand-strategic visions lead to different views about the right way to use violence in conflict. Officers align with different political champions who share their preferences, or they tailor military advice to match their own implicit theory of security. Campaign plans are subject to radical and abrupt change as military and political leaders come and go. Strategies that survive this culling process often do so by appealing to the lowest common denominator, acceptable but half-hearted compromises that are ultimately unsatisfying.

Such disappointments ought to be less likely when states can focus their efforts on one particular adversary. The presence of an especially dangerous rival should concentrate the mind. If grand strategists all agree about the main adversary, they should be able to arrive at some consensus about how to deal with it, and thus to ensure their own security. Such was the case, we are told, for the United States during the Cold War. For the better part of a half-century, US leaders fixated on the overriding danger of Soviet power. The Soviet Union may have been an existential threat, but for those responsible for conceiving and implementing grand strategy, it was also an analytical luxury.

The reality, however, was much more complex. Although policymakers agreed that the Soviet Union was the most important challenge for the US, there was profound and lasting disagreement about the nature of the challenge. Was it ideological or material? Was it military or economic? And which side had the advantage of time? Did the US need to act with a sense of urgency to preserve the post-war order, or could it adopt a more restrained posture, confident that the underlying sources of security and prosperity were on its side?

Two other issues divided grand strategists: the importance of peripheral conflicts, and the role of nuclear weapons. This chapter explores these divisive issues for grand strategy and shows how they influenced the theory and practice of US strategy. It also shows how a focus on strategy and grand strategy sheds new light on well-known historical controversies.

## Vietnam reconsidered

The US entered the Vietnam War to preserve the independence of the non-communist government in Saigon. A growing insurgency and conventional military pressure from the North put this goal at risk by the early 1960s, prompting some observers to warn of a political collapse and the rapid expansion of communist rule in Southeast Asia. US military personnel initially served as advisers before joining the fight directly. A modest expeditionary force soon turned into a large-scale ground presence, ultimately reaching about a half-million deployed personnel in 1968.

In addition to land operations, US air forces conducted increasingly ferocious bombing campaigns in support of ground operations, and to coerce the communists to settle the war on acceptable terms. Progress towards an endgame was agonisingly slow, and as the conflict dragged out in Vietnam, the war became politically radioactive at home. The Paris Peace Accords stopped the fighting in 1973, but only temporarily. Two years later the North Vietnamese army overran the South, unifying the country under communist rule. The US, despite its overwhelming advantages, lost.

Critics of US strategy in the war have stressed the military's preference for conventional operations. Instead of engaging in a proper counter-insurgency campaign, the army chose a tragically ill-suited war of attrition.[1] These arguments resonated for some strategists after the invasions of Afghanistan (2001) and Iraq (2003), when occupying ground forces seemed unprepared to fend off insurgent violence. Some military officers warned against indulging in conventional preferences, given the unconventional nature of the post-9/11 wars. Their warnings led to the publication of a high-profile counter-insurgency manual and deliberate efforts to avoid the mistakes of Vietnam. This time would be different.[2]

But the historical analogy was tenuous, because the US strategic failure in Vietnam was not really the result of combat preferences. US forces attempted a variety of approaches in the war, including both conventional and counter-insurgency campaigns. The disappointing outcome was not the result of operational myopia. The deeper issue was the lack of an intelligible grand strategy during the period of its major combat operations, in the years between the Cuban Missile Crisis and the eventual detente between the superpowers. The end of the crisis relieved some of the tension in US–Soviet relations and helped set in motion events that would culminate in detente at the end of the decade. But Cold War shibboleths died hard, especially in the Lyndon Johnson administration. The president was tormented by this question. He would have preferred that the Cuban denouement freed up his administration to focus on domestic policy, yet he couldn't shake the fear that losing in places like Vietnam would have terrible long-term effects on the US reputation for resolve. 'What the hell is Vietnam worth to me?', he pleaded to his national security advisor. 'What is it worth to this country?'[3]

The fact that grand strategy was in flux made it difficult to define victory. The nominal goal was preserving an independent South Vietnam, but no one could agree on how to measure South Vietnam's resiliency. Because there was no obvious standard for assessing Saigon's ability to survive without assistance, there was little consensus on when the US could safely withdraw. Observers also disagreed about the consequences of a possible collapse. Concerns about creeping communism and falling dominoes animated US grand strategy before the war, but the intelligence community challenged these assumptions as early as 1964.[4] The benefits of winning and the costs of losing were unclear even as the US was increasing its involvement. In the critical years of escalation, political and military leaders struggled to craft their approach to the war without a clear view of the meaning of victory and defeat.[5]

Disagreement about the purpose of the war led to piecemeal strategies and analytical confusion. Hedging came naturally for leaders who did not understand the relationship between victory and security. A loose version of the domino theory continued to hold sway in the Johnson administration, causing the president to worry that losing in Vietnam would foreshadow a string of defeats elsewhere. At the same time, a number of sceptics inside and outside government offered a more sanguine view, and they urged the White House not to commit to a conflict whose outcome would not directly implicate US security. Ferocious internecine fights about strategy in Vietnam reflected a deeper divide about the foundations of US grand strategy. That argument was never fully resolved.

\*　\*　\*

America's theory of security in the Cold War was an amalgam of duelling beliefs about containment. Two broad schools of thought developed in the early years of competition with the Soviet Union. One came from George Kennan, a diplomat and Russia specialist who popularised the idea of containment. His approach was based on a simple map of the Cold War that distinguished core areas from the periphery. For Kennan, core areas or 'strong points' were centres of industry and economic strength: the US, Western Europe, the Soviet Union, Japan and, because of its vast oil resources, the Persian Gulf. These were the only places with the latent economic capacity and military strength needed to compete in a long-term great-power competition. The periphery was everywhere else.[6]

This was a conservative and sanguine view of containment. The US and its partners controlled four of the five core areas in world politics, meaning that the balance of capabilities would remain in its favour. Moreover, US political institutions were stronger and more resilient than those in the Soviet Union. This meant that the US could practise patience, and it need not risk military interventions in peripheral places. Husbanding its resources and bolstering core partners was enough to preserve a favourable status quo. Over time, the Soviet Union would collapse under the weight of its dysfunctional authoritarian regime and its command economy.

US leaders were less sure, and they leaned towards a more ominous vision. From their perspective, the line between 'core' and 'periphery' was fuzzy and moveable. Failure to stand up to aggression, even in areas not immediately vital to US national security, might encourage more communist risk-taking. Restraint would also signal a lack of commitment to international institutions and the evolving liberal world order.[7] At the same time, officials sought to avoid a repeat of the Korean War, a costly stalemate and a cautionary tale about getting bogged down in peripheral conflicts. Every president from Dwight Eisenhower to Richard Nixon sought ways of confronting communist rivals without suffering the same fate. This was especially the case in Vietnam, where grand-strategic indecision had deep and lasting effects on wartime strategy.

Uncertain about the demands of containment in the aftermath of the Berlin and Cuban crises, policymakers looked for low-cost solutions that would allow them to sustain the status quo without paying an exorbitant price. This in part explains the allure of special-operations and foreign-military-advisory missions.[8] The use of elite forces to assist foreign friends made a great deal of sense for a country trying to sort out its grand-strategic priorities. This approach was not enough, however, given the Vietnamese communists' will to persist. Chronic corruption and political instability aggravated the problem, and as Vietnam descended into further violence, officials searched for new approaches, including US military action.[9]

Airpower was particularly appealing for policymakers in the Johnson administration who were committed to the cause but sensitive to the costs. It held two main attractions. Firstly, carefully calibrated strategic bombing offered an alternative to a large ground war, with all the costs and risks that would have entailed. Secondly, airpower advocates believed that the US could use bombing as a sophisticated tool of coercion.

Intense raids would be followed by strategic pauses, giving Hanoi an opportunity to think about the pain it was suffering and to worry about the next round. What Thomas Schelling called 'the diplomacy of violence' would allow Washington to convince North Vietnam to settle the war without having to spend too much on a conflict of questionable strategic value to the US.[10]

While there was some enthusiasm for airpower, the administration was wary of the type of bombing campaign that might provoke North Vietnam's great-power patrons. During the Korean War, China sent huge numbers of 'volunteers' to rescue Pyongyang, preventing its defeat and producing a bloody stalemate. Large-scale fighting between Chinese and American troops in Vietnam might have been even worse, especially after China joined the nuclear club in 1964. China supported North Vietnam financially and sent many advisers and thousands of railroad troops to assist in its defence, but it took steps to avoid overt confrontation with the US, and American leaders were keen to keep it that way. For these reasons, the administration sought to ratchet up the pressure slowly and sharply restricted the target list.[11]

Some air-force officers did not respond well to the administration's gradual escalation of the air campaign, viewing its risk aversion as deeply unwise. Service leaders came from a traditional and organisational culture favouring heavy bombing – or none at all.[12] The idea of limited wars was also anathema to air-force leaders who worried about their organisation's wealth, autonomy and prestige. No one worried so much as General Curtis LeMay, who led the Strategic Air Command (SAC) and served as chief of staff in the Johnson administration. 'In such wars', writes Marshall Michel, 'SAC's nuclear force was useless, SAC aircraft might be asked to operate outside of SAC's direct control, and such wars would have to be fought primarily by the other services and tactical air forces, with the concomitant diminishment of SAC's share of the defense budget'.[13] To the extent that air-force leaders thought about air strategy in limited wars, they only expressed a vague idea that bombers would be especially intimidating to US enemies. The air force continually pressed for heavy bombing raids, not so much because it had a clear idea of how that would compel enemies to come to terms, but because that was how the service thought airpower ought to be used.[14]

Despite the appeal of strategic bombing as a coercive tool, policymakers also had limited expectations about the coming air campaign in Vietnam. The bombing began as a way to relieve pressure on a fragile ally; a way of assisting a demoralised South Vietnamese army and bolstering the Saigon government.[15] At best the White House hoped that it would interrupt shipping from north to south and boost morale in Saigon.[16] The bombing was not intended to destroy the communists' ability to fight or compel a settlement – at least not at first. While the majority of Johnson's advisers supported the campaign, most of them did so simply because *something* was necessary to stop the bleeding. Others, including vice president Hubert Humphrey, were outspoken in opposition, arguing that the bombing campaign was unlikely to affect Hanoi's calculations but would impel the US towards deeper involvement in the war.[17]

The Johnson administration tried to articulate its rationale. A working group in late 1964 considered options for the campaign, including an intensive bombing programme that would be coupled with a demand for unconditional surrender and proof that the North had stopped aid to the insurgency in the South. This option was rejected, however, on the grounds that it would be difficult to do enough damage to an agrarian economy to compel such a decision, and because the risk of escalation was too high.

The working group also suggested a more limited alternative that would increase bombing but pause it once negotiations began. There was not much enthusiasm for this approach because, as the group put it, 'at best ... [North Vietnam] might feign compliance and settle for an opportunity to subvert the South another day'.[18] Nonetheless, this became the default position, both because the administration could control the scope and pace of the campaign and because it presented the least risk of horizontal escalation.

The president's advisers continued to disagree about its goals after the campaign started in earnest. Summarising the results of the first several months of bombing, secretary of defense Robert McNamara argued that it had been worthwhile inasmuch as it capped the North's ability to resupply the insurgency, but he acknowledged that it was not a warwinner. 'I do not believe that even a greatly expanded program of bombing could be expected to produce a significant North Vietnamese interest in a negotiated solution', he concluded, 'until they have been disappointed in their hopes for a quick military success in the South'.[19]

Unable to agree on strategic questions, the administration immersed itself in tactics. Caught between the attraction of coercive airpower and the fear of Chinese intervention, policymakers obsessed over daily targeting decisions. Clark Clifford, the chair of the President's Foreign Intelligence Advisory Board, offered a telling description of the Johnson White House:

> Exhausted, harassed, besieged men found it necessary to concentrate on tactics rather than strategy, on micro-problems rather than macro-solutions, on today's crises rather than tomorrow's opportunities. New bombing target 'packages' rather than diplomatic or political initiatives tended to be the typical

menu for the President's 'Tuesday Lunch.' Someone once said (about LBJ) … 'If you told him right now of a sure-fire way to defeat the Viet Cong and to get out of Vietnam, he would groan that he was too busy to worry about that now; he had to discuss next week's bombing targets.'[20]

The administration had no sure-fire way of defeating the insurgency; indeed, officials could not agree on what it meant to win. But withdrawing from the conflict was not an option as long as the fear of falling dominoes lingered. Frustrated by the lack of progress, the White House subsequently expanded the target set to include strikes on oil-storage facilities, industry and electric power, though the lack of industrial targets meant that the campaign still primarily focused on interdiction. By 1968, Johnson approved requests to strike targets closer to urban centres for the purpose of damaging morale and forcing North Vietnam to negotiate a settlement. While he loosened some restrictions, however, he still took steps to avoid the kind of campaign that might provoke overt Chinese entry. The results were disappointing, and civil–military antagonism persisted.[21]

The Nixon administration escalated the bombing of North Vietnam, ordering two major campaigns in 1972. The first lasted from May–October and focused on North Vietnam's transportation and energy infrastructure. US planes dropped 155,548 tonnes of bombs during the spring and summer alone. The campaign successfully targeted the North's rail network, increasing the time and cost of sending supplies to the South. Despite these tactical successes, however, the campaign had little lasting impact on the North's capability because it had prepositioned stockpiles in the South and was able to transition its resupply effort from rail to road.[22] The next campaign, in contrast, was geared more towards signalling US resolve than destroying the North Vietnamese army's capabilities. Following months of sluggish peace talks, the White House authorised raids against Hanoi and other targets to force it to agree to South Vietnamese demands for a revised agreement. The campaign appeared to pay dividends: negotiators finally reached a settlement in January 1973.

This turn in the war seemed to validate critics who had blamed the Johnson White House for micromanagement and risk aversion. The US might have won the war, according to this argument, if only the administration had unleashed the air force earlier. Beginning in the 1980s, however, airpower historians started to heap criticism on the air force for its stubborn commitment to strategic bombing. Interestingly, the strongest critiques came from former officers, who thought that the service bore as much responsibility for the outcome as the White House. According to Earl Tilford, for example, the air force cultivated the myth that civilian leaders kept them from implementing what would have been an effective strategy. In fact, they had none. The air force

> could not – and did not – develop a strategy appropriate to the war at hand. In fact, they failed to articulate any coherent strategy at all. In Vietnam the Air Force fell victim to its own brief history and to the unswerving commitment of its leadership to the dubious doctrine of strategic bombing.[23]

The argument here challenges both interpretations. It is not clear that a major bombing campaign would have done much good early in the war. North Vietnam was only vulnerable because of the combined effects of the Tet Offensive in 1968, which devastated the southern insurgency, and the Easter Offensive in 1971, which devastated the North Vietnamese army.[24] More importantly, the outcome of the air war would not have been much different, even if the air force had been creative and nimble. Graduated airpower escalation was a seductive strategy because it seemed to resolve an uncertain grand strategy. There is no reason to believe policymakers would have chosen differently had the air force been less committed to strategic bombing. There is also no reason to believe a more competent campaign of graduated escalation would have affected North Vietnam's calculus, given its demonstrated willingness to absorb punishment.

The shift in strategy in the later bombing campaigns reflected a broader shift in grand strategy. The Johnson administration made key strategic decisions in the transitional years between the peak of Cold War tensions and the peak of detente. Grand strategy came into focus in the Nixon administration, which stressed a return to realpolitik rather than a zero-sum version of containment. The White House pursued detente with both the Soviet Union and China in order to exploit the rift between them in a way that would encourage long-term change in their behaviour. Both sides saw reasons to come closer to the US. This was especially the case for China, which perceived a serious threat from the Soviet Union and was reeling from its own Cultural Revolution. Nixon's approach to the communist great powers had the effect of isolating North Vietnam, which reduced the risk of expanding the bombing campaign.[25] By the end of 1972 the North had emptied its stockpile of SA-2 surface-to-air missiles, and it had no indigenous production capability.[26]

The shift in US grand strategy opened new opportunities for coercive bombing. Extending a hand to Beijing put Hanoi on the horns of a dilemma, because it could not be sure of continued support from its great-power patron. Under these circumstances, it was much more sensitive to the material cost of US bombing efforts, and it had reason to seek a negotiated peace.

\*   \*   \*

Grand-strategic uncertainty also led to a fight over strategy on the ground. During the war and after, this debate pitted advocates of conventional action against advocates of population-centric counter-insurgency. Some contend the army's organisational and cultural biases caused it to relentlessly pursue conventional military operations against an unconventional enemy. This, to critics, was the root cause of failure.[27] Others argue that by the early 1970s, the army had improved its conventional approach and incorporated the right blend of military violence and political action. The problem, from this perspective, was that leaders were slow to recognise how far it had come.[28] Although the Nixon administration expanded the war into Cambodia in the 1970s, critics contend that it missed opportunities to expand the war in ways that would have hobbled the communist effort.[29]

Policymakers were reluctant to fully invest in either kind of campaign. Conventional fighting and counter-insurgency both evolved in fits and starts. In the early phase of US involvement, proposals to invade North Vietnam or Laos were not seriously considered. One problem was the practical difficulty involved in expanding the theatre of operations, especially if the goal was interdicting the movement of supplies across a vast region. Expanding the ground war would also potentially make US troops more vulnerable and isolated. But the practical problems of conventional war did not mean that counter-insurgency would be any easier. Indeed, some of the same problems plagued large-scale pacification and rural-development efforts central to the counter-insurgency approach. This would involve locating and evict-ing insurgents from far-flung hamlets and staying in sufficient numbers to provide security and assist with economic development and local institution-building. The effort would also require deep inter-agency coordination and close cooperation between civilian and military officials.

More important than these practical considerations were the costs in time, manpower and money. A fully committed war effort did not logically flow from Johnson's ambiguous grand strategy, meaning he would have been reticent to adopt more ambitious strategies even if he was utterly persuaded by the strategic logic of expanding the ground war or investing more in counter-insurgency.

During the summer of 1965, when Johnson was weighing a military request for a substantial increase in US forces, he received a series of position papers from key advisers: George Ball, McGeorge Bundy, William Bundy and Robert McNamara. These revealed basic disagreements about whether the US should fight at all, and if so with how many troops. Other infor-mal advisers warned the president that a deeper investment could lead to disaster. Clark Clifford put the matter directly in a letter to Johnson:

> My concern is that a substantial buildup of US ground troops would be construed by the Communists, and by the world, as a determination on our part to win the war on the ground. This could be a quagmire. It could turn into an open end commitment on our part that would take more and more ground troops, without a realistic hope of ultimate victory.[30]

The president ultimately sided with those arguing for bolstering the US presence. Ball observed an 'agonizing reluctance to go forward', and Johnson tried to pre-emptively put a cap on escalation and keep his options open. Indeed, even as Johnson was acceding to requests to increase the number of troops in summer 1965, he was arguing privately that he would not go too far. 'I don't think I should go over 100,000 but I think I should go to that number and explain it', he relayed to George Ball. 'I told McNamara that I would not make a decision on this and not to assume that I am willing to go overboard on this. I ain't.'[31]

Johnson did expand the ground war, of course, but even during the period of escalation he remained wary of taking the fight outside South Vietnam. Instead, the administration settled on a strategy of attrition, on the loose strategic logic that the path to victory would become clear if US and South Vietnamese military forces could eliminate enemy fighters faster than they could be replaced. Because North Vietnam could not sustain the insurgency when it passed this 'crossover point', it would be amenable to a settlement. While the administration never explicitly described the logic connecting higher attrition rates to coercive success, it saw several virtues in the approach. For instance, it made the bombing campaign more politically acceptable because leaders could argue that eroding North Vietnam's logistics would make resupply harder and thus accelerate the march towards the crossover point. It also allowed the administration to exploit the United States' comparative advantages in technology and firepower.[32]

In short, the attrition war was feasible though suboptimal, and in theory it was less costly than the alternatives. Expanding the ground war risked much higher US casualties, especially if China intervened. Expanding the counter-insurgency risked a very long engagement on behalf of an ally who was supposed to learn how to survive without US aid. The strategy itself, however, was based more on wishful thinking than a clear idea of how attrition would succeed against an enemy that had already demonstrated the willingness to suffer a staggering number of casualties. For this reason, some policymakers and military leaders saw the attrition war as futile, and the search for alternatives became hostile and divisive.

Just as there was no consensus on the strategy, there was no consensus on appropriate measures of effectiveness. Some sought to apply operations-research methods to the war, believing that the systematic collection and analysis of data would 'sharpen the combat edge'.[33] Critics responded by arguing that the army was stubbornly trying to wage a counter-guerrilla war without having to abandon its conventional biases. Conventional measures were meaningless in a counter-insurgency, the critics claimed, where what was most important were intangible indicators about civilians' sense of security and the government's claim to legitimacy. At a deeper level, the fixation on statistical measures of progress like relative casualty rates suggested the amorality of the war itself and the army's naive belief that it could kill its way to victory.[34] These criticisms went too far. Despite accusations about the army's myopia, in reality it attempted a hodgepodge of measures to try to get a grasp of progress in the war. Indeed, one historian argues that it ended up with a motley and unmanageable set of metrics.[35] The problem was not a dogmatic attachment to old-fashioned conventional doctrine, but the lack of any clear way to gauge the results of conventional combat. This was a direct result of the fact that there was no clear strategic goal, no benchmark upon which to deploy reasonable measures.

Pacification was similarly fraught. Given the dismal state of Vietnam's economy and endemic political instability, rural reconstruction and development was a very expensive proposition. Committing to the task meant many years of continued investment and occupation. In addition, the debate over pacification revealed deep divisions about the nature of the war. As a result, pacification advocates faced serious opposition, and some of the most intense criticism came from within government. Notably, the debate reached its climax after the US had built its peak troop level in Vietnam, an indication of profound strategic discord.

In late 1966 Robert Komer, a key Johnson adviser who would go on to lead the pacification effort, circulated a strategic plan for the following year. The plan was particularly important because it represented a call for the government to coordinate its military, intelligence and diplomatic programmes for the purpose of state-building at the local level. According to his biographer, Komer's proposal was a 'feasible, acceptable, and suitable counterinsurgency designed to take possession of the strategic initiative rather than react to Hanoi'.[36] But his plan met heavy resistance across the board, and it was rejected by the Pentagon, the State Department, the military command in Vietnam, the Joint Chiefs of Staff, Pacific Command and the US embassy. Komer believed that opposition to his ideas was fuelled by 'prideful creatures in the bureaucratic jungles of Washington and Saigon', and he set about convincing the president to grant him more power to reshape American strategy. He largely succeeded, and he used his presidential mandate to browbeat both military and civilian officials in Vietnam to join the pacification campaign. Nonetheless, he always blamed inter-agency politics for the shortcomings in the US effort.[37]

This explanation downplays the serious questions raised by his critics. Pacification required a dedicated military effort to 'clear and hold' civilian areas in order to buy time for political and economic development. Neither South Vietnamese nor US commanders were enthusiastic about this effort, however, because it meant diverting combat units from offensive operations and pinning them down indefinitely.[38] Such a diversion was especially pointless after the Tet Offensive, they argued, when the insurgents presented a comparatively small security threat. General William Westmoreland later referred to the insurgency as a 'nuisance' and 'not a serious threat to the regime'. He was uncomfortable with the fact that he 'received pressure to put emphasis on pacification at the risk of allowing the main force to have a free rein'.[39]

Komer's great success was in persuading the president that the war was fundamentally about politics and psychology. He believed that attrition was important, but only insofar as it greased the wheels for pacification. Everything depended on civilians' perception of internal security and governmental competence. These criteria required fewer tangible measures of effectiveness, however, and not everyone was ready to jettison their existing quantitative measures. Doing so would mean acknowledging that the United States was involved in a radically different war. The emphasis on measuring the relative strength of the North Vietnamese army and the communist insurgency, as opposed to focusing on progress in civil affairs, flowed from the belief that the US was the defender in a war of aggression. Changing the metrics meant redefining the conflict as a kind of violent electoral campaign nested within a broader civil war. Again, it is worth emphasising that no one could agree on the nature of the war during the most intense period of combat. This made coherent strategy impossible.[40]

The deep divisions about whether and how to fight also led to contradictory approaches, as key officials tried to juggle countervailing pressures in Vietnam and Washington. Komer was dubious of quantifying pacification, for example, but he also recognised the need to deliver hard data to overcome scepticism at home. His solution was to send regular updates from the Hamlet Evaluation System, a detailed monthly and quarterly survey of a host of indicators, including everything from statistics on security to the state of schools and the local economy.[41] The danger of using the system, of course, was that Komer was setting a precedent for something that was allergic to quantification, and would in turn mislead policymakers and the public about the results of the US effort.

A more important contradiction had to do with moral hazard. Komer and others believed that Saigon would have to take the lead in order for pacification to work. This was eminently reasonable, given the notion that victory in the war would only be reached when the host government could stand on its own. Nonetheless, the plan required a massive long-term US programme for securing the Vietnamese countryside and improving the lives of Vietnamese civilians. Thus, by convincing Johnson that the US should obligate itself to the dual tasks of pacification and rural development, he was inadvertently signalling to Vietnamese leaders that they need not bother.

\* \* \*

Covert action was a third option for policymakers who were not convinced of the strategic value of Vietnam but were not ready to abandon the field. It was vanishingly cheap in comparison to conventional or counter-insurgency warfare, and it was a relatively low-risk proposition. Because covert action meant that the US could plausibly deny its involvement in specific operations, it could feign ignorance in order to avoid direct confrontations with the communist great powers. Plausible deniability was particularly attractive to policymakers, who were using the rhetoric of democracy in the Cold War ideological contest, but who were also willing to support an illiberal regime in Saigon.

The covert war failed. Incursions into North Vietnam proved disastrous and tragic. South Vietnamese commandos trained as covert operatives were often discovered shortly after crossing into the North, and their efforts produced little of value. Small-scale CIA efforts were eclipsed by a more comprehensive military effort led by the Studies and Observation Group, but the results were disappointing despite the additional resources.[42] Nonetheless, policymakers, intelligence officials and special-operations officers were reluctant to give up, despite increasing evidence that covert initiatives were hopeless.

Covert action is self-limiting, which makes US enthusiasm in Vietnam especially puzzling. The number of personnel involved has to remain small in order to maintain operational secrecy and plausible deniability, but this reduces what it can accomplish. In addition, covert operations require exquisite intelligence to overcome the limitations in size and resources, but espionage and action work at cross-purposes, because action alerts the target and makes continued collection more difficult. Finally, the revelation of covert actions can have serious domestic consequences. Policymakers and intelligence officials who try to keep their actions hidden look especially sinister, even if those actions are relatively benign.

Covert action is especially hard against a committed enemy that puts a premium on counter-intelligence, as was the case in Vietnam, and neither the CIA nor MAC-V SOG (Military Assistance Command, Vietnam – Studies and Observations Group) was able to do much against what was effectively a police state. Worse, revelations of covert action blew back on the agency and policymakers. The *Phoenix Program*, for example, became shorthand for a notorious killing campaign, even though it served a host of other purposes, and even though vastly more civilians and combatants were killed in overt military campaigns. The fact that *Phoenix* was covert made it look suspicious.[43]

Be that as it may, covert action proved to be irresistible. White House, State Department and military officials saw practical benefits. They used covert action to improve intelligence collection, and they hoped that cross-border incursions might inhibit the flow of war materials to insurgents in the South.[44] More important, however, was their belief that covert actions were a way of sending subtle messages to Hanoi that simultaneously signalled US commitment to protecting South Vietnam but also a desire not to let the war spin out of control. State Department analysts speculated that the communist regime might view US actions as tacit threats of more 'militant, active measures'.[45] At the same time, the fact that they were not claiming responsibility signalled to the communist great powers their desire to limit the conflict.

Officials clung to covert action, despite the operational failures and political risks, because they were desperate for a low-cost way to fight the war. The stakes in Vietnam were unclear because American grand strategy was ambiguous. Thus policymakers were reluctant to invest in high-cost strategies and quick to gravitate towards low-cost solutions, even if they held out little hope of success.

*   *   *

Two broad conclusions follow from this analysis. Firstly, the ongoing debates about the 'right' doctrine in Vietnam obscure the deeper problem in the war. Because the Johnson administration had no firm grand strategy, it was unable to forge a consensus about what kind of victory was acceptable. Implementing a rational strategy was impossible under these conditions. The ferocious arguments about army choices (big-unit war versus

counter-insurgency) and air-force options (graduated escalation or rapidly expanding the bombing campaign) did not
really reflect controversies over doctrine. Instead, they reflected
strategic incoherence at the highest levels. Secondly, grand strategies affect more than just decisions about force structure, force
posture and the decision for war. They also affect the quality
of strategy in war and decisions about how to fight. Similarly,
the lack of a grand strategy can lead to frustration and failure
among military officers who face the unenviable task of planning a war without a clear notion of the objective.

US grand strategy in the 1960s was caught between the
lingering fear of falling dominoes and the profound desire to
avoid new confrontations with communist rivals. During the
pivotal years of US involvement, no one could answer Lyndon
Johnson's question about the Vietnam War – 'What is it worth
to this country?' – in a way that satisfied all the parties with a
stake in the outcome. Deep uncertainty about grand strategy
had pernicious consequences for wartime strategy. US indecision was compounded by other features of Cold War politics,
and chief among them was the special fear of nuclear weapons.

## Strategy, grand strategy and the nuclear revolution

Bernard Brodie famously described the strategic consequences
of nuclear weapons shortly after Hiroshima and Nagasaki.
'Thus far', he wrote, 'the chief purpose of our military establishment has been to win wars. From now on its chief purpose
must be to avert them. It can have almost no other useful
purpose.'[46] Anticipating proliferation to the Soviet Union,
Brodie tried to imagine the possible utility of great-power war
among nuclear powers. He found none. There was no way
of achieving the state's political purposes when the consequences of war included the end of the state as a functioning
political entity. Possession of nuclear weapons might deter

foreign rivals from invasion, but the idea of wartime use for coercion was a grotesque logical absurdity. This idea was revolutionary. States had a lot of experience incorporating military innovations in their war-fighting plans and they had powerful reasons to welcome new tools that improved the chance of victory. Now they had mastered the ultimate weapon and they couldn't use it.[47]

US leaders, however, consistently rejected these ideas. Instead of viewing nuclear weapons solely as tools of deterrence, they sought new technologies and techniques that might enable nuclear use for political gain. Leaders were particularly impressed by the notion that improvements in nuclear war-fighting capabilities would ultimately benefit deterrence. Critics of the nuclear revolution identified what they saw as a major logical shortcoming of the theory. Nuclear-armed states needed to be able to tell a story to their adversaries about how they might use nuclear weapons in war. If adversaries did not believe the story, then nuclear threats were meaningless. But if states could claim that they had figured out how to fight at a reasonable cost – and if their rivals believed them – then their deterrent threats would carry real weight. Doing so, of course, required demonstrating new technological innovations, including highly accurate warheads, reliable surveillance platforms, effective command and control, and robust defences. It also required promulgating doctrine to adversaries and allies alike about how they might use these new technologies in war.[48]

US leaders set out to do all those things. They invested in a staggering array of nuclear weapons, many of which were explicitly designed for battlefield use. They also invested in exotic satellite technologies that would enable better warning intelligence and more precise targeting data. They spent decades helping the armed forces build capabilities for locating and tracking Soviet submarines, bombers and missiles.

And as the Cold War went on, they developed more sophisticated approaches to war fighting. From early visions of massive
retaliation in response to even limited Soviet aggression, US
strategists wrote much more detailed descriptions about how
they would employ nuclear weapons in different scenarios.
Analysts engaged in furious debates about whether such plans
were realistic and necessary for deterrence, or whether they
were dangerous fantasies. These debates were never resolved.
But for our purposes, what matters is that policymakers were
usually interested. They were never willing to take Brodie's
admonition as gospel. In fact, they were usually more inclined
to reject it.[49]

The theory of nuclear revolution also failed to explain
leaders' fear of proliferation. If the logic of mutually assured
destruction inspired sobriety all around, then they ought to
have been sanguine about the spread of nuclear weapons.
Instead, US leaders worried that proliferation would spin out
of control, and they spent decades trying to prevent it. They
coerced, cajoled and bribed their allies to resist the impulse to
go nuclear. They built and sustained international institutions
devoted to watching for evidence of proliferation, and they
crafted international treaties that rewarded states for keeping
their nuclear aspirations at bay. US diplomats discussed war-
fighting doctrine with allies to convince them that the US could
extend deterrence without risking universal destruction. And
in some cases, US officials quietly discussed clandestine joint
efforts with other nuclear-armed states against third parties
whom they feared were pursuing their own arsenals.[50]

The nuclear-revolution theory is inconsistent with the history
of US grand strategy in the Cold War. If the theory held sway, we
would have seen very different policy choices. US leaders would
have restricted the size, cost and complexity of the nuclear arsenal.
They would have isolated nuclear weapons from conventional

forces rather than integrating nuclear options into war-fighting plans. They would have focused less on non-proliferation and allowed nuclear weapons to spread, confident that the logic of universal deterrence would lead to global stability. But the historical record reveals something else entirely. Officials were never comfortable with the logic of the nuclear revolution, and they spent decades looking for alternatives.

\*   \*   \*

The theory, however, fares better in terms of strategy. The Cold War witnessed grotesque military violence, but leaders were remarkably cautious when it came to nuclear weapons. They used their arsenals for coercive purposes, to be sure, and they invested a great deal of thought into how they might use them in war. But when presented with the opportunity to translate those ideas into action, they retreated. Indeed, the same leaders who were quite aggressive with conventional arms became surprisingly cautious when given the opportunity to use nuclear weapons. Because modern history would be so different if leaders had not been so cautious, their reluctance to escalate demands an explanation. Perhaps they were rationally terrified of reprisals in kind, and this fear overwhelmed all other considerations at the moment of truth. Perhaps they were morally repulsed by the idea, especially given the jaw-dropping estimates of civilian deaths in a hypothetical nuclear exchange. Perhaps they could not bear the psychological weight of breaking the nuclear taboo. Some mix of these emotions might have served as a powerful barrier to catastrophe. Despite having many opportunities to use nuclear weapons in anger, they consistently rejected the idea.

Cold War leaders refused operational plans requiring nuclear pre-emption. American presidents, Republican and Democrat alike, spoke in ways that suggested they could never bring themselves to launch nuclear weapons. President Harry S. Truman did not regret his decision to use the bomb at the end of the Second World War, though even at the time he sensed that the implications went beyond normal strategic judgement. 'I fear that machines are ahead of morals by some centuries', he wrote in his diary on the first atomic test in July 1945, 'and when morals catch up, perhaps there'll be no reason for any of it. I hope not.' Existential dread permeated his public speeches as well. As he put it in his final State of the Union Address:

> We have entered the atomic age, and war has undergone a technological change which makes it a very different thing from what it used to be. War today between the Soviet empire and the free nations might dig the grave not only of our Stalinist opponents, but of our own society, or world as well as theirs ... The war of the future would be one in which man could ... destroy the very structure of a civilization that has been slowly and painfully built up through hundreds of generations. Such a war is not a possible policy for rational men.[51]

President Eisenhower expressed similar views about the strategic and moral implications of nuclear war, especially after the advent of vastly more powerful thermonuclear weapons. In August 1955 Eisenhower told the National Security Council that 'the nature of conflict has gotten beyond man'. Speaking bluntly, he promised that 'if this is the only means of waging war, he would never wage it'.[52] President John F. Kennedy was appalled by the prospect of escalation, seeing it as morally intolerable and strategically self-defeating, and he searched during his short presidency for lesser means of confronting the Soviet Union. After receiving a report on the effect of nuclear weapons, he told secretary of state Dean Rusk, 'and we call ourselves the human race'.[53]

During the Vietnam War, defence analysts pondered the use of tactical nuclear weapons against a variety of targets, but no American leader took the idea seriously.[54] President Nixon briefly pondered the use of strategic nuclear threats to compel an end to the war, apparently believing that cultivating a reputation as a 'madman' would scare US enemies into settling the conflict rather than taking their chances. He did not, however, seriously entertain the idea of following through on the bluff, which was in any case ineffective.[55] The fact that the White House recognised nuclear-escalation threats as a sign of madness suggests that there is something to the theory of the nuclear revolution – at least at the level of strategy.

Soviet leaders, from Stalin onwards, also mixed public bluster with private reservations. When Truman casually informed Stalin about 'a new weapon of unusual destructive force', Stalin responded with equally casual enthusiasm, encouraging the American president to put it to use against Japan.[56] Stalin's perspective, in this sense, was akin to Eisenhower's early declaration that the bomb was simply a larger weapon. Yet the news of Hiroshima and Nagasaki had a powerful impact on the Soviet dictator, who turned his attention – and the resources of the state – towards the development of a Soviet nuclear programme.[57] He clearly believed that nuclear weapons were important for resisting US coercion, though the exact ways in which they would affect Soviet grand strategy were as yet unclear.

We know less about Stalin's views about nuclear weapons and wartime strategy, though there are some indications that he was unwilling to risk escalation. As Sergey Radchenko observes:

Time and again in postwar crises he raised the temperature only to back off when faced with US resolve. He did so in August 1945, when he attempted to land forces on Hokkaido, in Japan, only to back down in the face of Truman's opposition. He did it again in March 1946 when, after a show of strength, he backed out of Iran. He did it most clearly during the Berlin blockade of 1948–49 when Stalin never gave the order to fire on the American planes that maintained the lifeline to West Berlin.[58]

Nikita Khrushchev was similarly misleading about his true views of the bomb. His public braggadocio was not consistent with his private recognition of the limits of brinkmanship and the absolute futility of nuclear use. In 1953 a special film was made for Soviet officials on the effects of nuclear weapons. His response, like Kennedy's, was shock and dismay. For a leader who had witnessed some of the most atrocious bloodlettings of the twentieth century, nuclear weapons still inspired a different kind of fear. The film left him 'depressed' and 'agitated'.[59] As Khrushchev told a reporter later:

When I was appointed First Secretary of the Central Committee [in 1953] and learned all the facts about nuclear power I couldn't sleep for several days. Then I became convinced that we could never possibly use these weapons, and when I realised that I was able to sleep again.[60]

Although he saw diplomatic value in blustering, he backed down from his threats in Berlin in 1961, and then again in Cuba in 1962. The latter case is particularly interesting, because recent historical evidence shows that Khrushchev had decided to de-escalate in Cuba only three days after the crisis began. His decision was less a response to American signals than a revelation of his true beliefs about the folly of nuclear use. According to a senior Soviet official present at key meetings during the crisis, Khrushchev 'shitted his pants' after learning that the US had moved its nuclear readiness to one level short of war.[61] For all his public swaggering, the first secretary could not bear the thought of crossing the nuclear threshold.

Soviet leaders remained cautious even after building their own enormous arsenal in the 1960s. When presented with estimates about the effects of a nuclear war in Europe, Soviet general secretary Leonid Brezhnev reportedly went pale.[62] Like Truman, Eisenhower, Khrushchev and Kennedy, he struggled to comprehend the consequences of a nuclear exchange. It was one thing to deploy nuclear weapons as a general deterrent against aggression or as a tool for bargaining and alliance diplomacy, and quite another to ponder their use in war. Nuclear weapons may have been useful tools for grand strategy, but they were absurd and terrifying as instruments of war.

Nuclear weapons had mixed effects on international politics during the Cold War, and it did not change as much as some early observers had expected. Yet in one sense they were revolutionary: leaders were unwilling to use them, despite universal recognition of their killing power. This is a first in the history of technology and war. No other weapons have inspired such caution.

\* \* \*

The nuclear shadow continues to loom over great-power politics. Over the last two decades, the US, China and Russia have all invested in modernisation programmes. They have replaced old warheads, deployed new missiles and platforms, and integrated advanced sensors into their nuclear systems.[63] They have also reinvigorated efforts to integrate nuclear operations with conventional military plans, suggesting that they envision a role for nuclear weapons in future conflicts. Put differently, they have all decided to spend a great deal of time and skill and money on war-fighting tools that no one has been willing to use for 80 years. Distinguishing strategy and grand strategy helps explain this apparent contradiction.

In the US, for example, advocates of nuclear modernisation argue that policy should not be constrained by the theory of the nuclear revolution. Not only does the theory fail to explain the actions of the Cold War superpowers, but it ignores the peacetime benefits of a modern arsenal. Matthew Kroenig, for instance, argues that nuclear superiority enhances bargaining leverage in crises. According to Kroenig, successful crisis diplomacy in the nuclear age is a competition in risk tolerance. States are more willing to run risks if they have more and better weapons at their disposal.[64] A large and reliable nuclear arsenal is also necessary for deterring regional great-power rivals, because it enables the US to extend deterrence over regional allies. US grand strategy, which seeks to extend the post-war liberal international order, ultimately depends on US nuclear promises.[65]

Critics of nuclear modernisation, however, focus on the strategic level. From their perspective, peacetime nuclear posturing is both pointless and dangerous. It is pointless because rational leaders will never follow through. It is dangerous because irrational leaders might. In a crisis, careful calculation may be overwhelmed by stress and confusion, making calamity possible.[66] In a war, contingency and chance may conspire against efforts to keep the conflict limited. As Charles Glaser writes, 'a large conventional war could escalate in numerous unpredictable ways, both planned and inadvertent, to full-scale strategic nuclear war'.[67] Inadvertent escalation may occur, for example, if nuclear and conventional forces are collocated or share the same command-and-control infrastructure.[68] Such 'entanglement' is more likely if states indulge the belief that nuclear weapons can play an important role in conventional military operations.[69]

Finally, strategy and grand strategy shed light on US–China competition. The ongoing debate about the implications of China's nuclear modernisation is in an important sense the latest iteration of the debate between nuclear-revolution theorists and their critics.[70] One group of analysts is relatively relaxed about China's efforts to improve the quality and increase the quantity of its nuclear weapons. These analysts rely on the logic of the revolution thesis. From their perspective, China's new investments are efforts to restore their deterrent capability in response to earlier US innovations. Washington, after all, spent many years developing its intelligence capabilities to improve targeting, and many resources on warhead and missile design to improve accuracy. Collectively, these efforts hint that a first strike might be possible. China's modernisation, seen in this light, is a rational response to US advances and a clear effort to restore deterrence.[71]

Not everyone is so sanguine. A second group of analysts see China's efforts as profoundly troubling. Rather than revealing a desire to restore deterrence, they foreshadow an attempt to use superior theatre nuclear forces to gain coercive leverage over the US and its allies and partners. From their perspective, and sharply deviating from the nuclear-revolution thesis, Chinese regional nuclear superiority will be a tool that Beijing can use to pry the US alliance apart, and a powerful bargaining instrument for coercing neighbouring countries. Nuclear weapons are not simply a means of deterring attack, but a powerful means of bullying smaller Asian states and expanding Chinese influence in the region.[72]

A third group of analysts focuses less on the nuclear balance per se, and more on the ways in which China's nuclear force affects conventional military operations. The danger, from this perspective, is that China is more likely to take conventional risks under the cover of its own nuclear umbrella. Chinese leaders may have no intention of using nuclear weapons, but their existence poses a threat for US leaders considering coming to the aid of regional partners under duress. As a result, Chinese efforts to assure retaliation by modernising its arsenal are not likely to increase stability, as nuclear-revolution theorists predict. Instead, they are likely to raise the risk of war. Borrowing from a different theoretical tradition, they worry that nuclear stability creates instability at lower levels. If two great powers feel sure that their forces can withstand attack, they may feel confident that they can fight a conventional war without risking everything. The twist in this case is that the US and China might not be equally sure about the ability to prevent nuclear escalation in a conventional war. US leaders have frequently expressed concern over escalation, deliberate or inadvertent, as we have seen in the Russia–Ukraine war. If China is less concerned, then a one-sided stability–instability paradox may result. Beijing would feel confident about controlling escalation; Washington would not. Under these conditions, China would have powerful incentives to force a resolution on the Taiwan issue, and the US would be reluctant to intervene.[73]

None of this is to argue that the US will abandon its friends and steer clear of its rivals in the case of war. Indeed, none of us can know exactly what US leaders will do in the heat of the moment. Ambiguity about future behaviour is baked into the US–China stand-off, an issue I treat in more detail in the last chapter. For now, it is enough to highlight the ways in which grand strategy and strategy interact in a hypothetical future conflict.

*   *   *

Reconstructing the Cold War can feel like making sense of the nonsensical. Two superpowers capable of mutual annihilation faced off in a decades-long ideological contest, both sides committed to prevailing but also perplexed by the problems they had created. Leaders who rose to power in the Cold War sometimes expressed a grim bewilderment about post-war geopolitics. Why should they risk the end of the world over other people's civil wars? Why should they sacrifice thousands of troops in faraway places with no obvious or immediate security implications? How could they fight against fierce enemies without letting violence spin out of control, especially given domestic doubts about the value of the war itself? Finally, why should they build thousands of weapons of mass destruction that they could barely imagine using?

Distinguishing strategy and grand strategy helps shed light on these questions. It helps explain the underlying reason why the American war in Vietnam was so frustrating. American grand strategy was in flux during the period of major conventional escalation. The most intense ground warfare occurred between the Cuban Missile Crisis and detente, leaving policymakers unsure about the value of ideological contests on the periphery of the Cold War. Although the White House still believed in protecting noncommunist partners against communist insurgents, the Cuban experience was a bracing reminder of the dangers of foreign interventions. The result in Vietnam was uncertainty about the appropriate strategy, civil–military tension, inter-agency squabbling and no consensus about the meaning of victory. The conventional wisdom about the war focuses on mismatched operational concepts and strategic requirements, but the deeper source of trouble was the wobbly bridge between strategy and grand strategy.

This distinction also reconciles the enduring puzzle over nuclear weapons. Recent scholarship has taken aim at the 'theory of the nuclear revolution', which holds that the peculiar characteristics of nuclear weapons should lead to small arsenals, limited defences and a relatively relaxed attitude towards proliferation. The superpowers did not behave this way in the Cold War, however. They built large and variegated nuclear arsenals, they invested in extensive air and missile defences, and they obsessed about the spread of nuclear weapons. That said, their attitude about *using* nuclear weapons was far different from their position on conventional weapons. Cold War leaders rejected nuclear use as immoral and self-defeating. They had many opportunities to escalate crises and war, but they chose restraint every time. Their reluctance suggests that nuclear weapons were indeed revolutionary, at least in this sense. Put another way, the theory of the nuclear revolution fails the historical test at the level of grand strategy, but passes at the level of strategy.

Questions about unconventional war and unconventional weapons are not a thing of the past. Quite the opposite: they animate the major disputes over policy and war since 9/11. The relationship between strategy and grand strategy helps put them in context, as I show in the following chapter.

## CHAPTER FOUR

# Strategy and grand strategy after September 11

The United States sent hundreds of thousands of men and women to fight in Afghanistan. It was never entirely clear what they were fighting for or whether they had any prospect of winning. Those who deployed repeatedly expressed deep frustration about the mission. Some lamented the dismal conditions in Afghanistan that provide fuel to seemingly endless violence.[1] Some spent years trying to make sense of missions that felt utterly futile.[2] Others felt actively deceived by policymakers and military leaders who offered rosy public pronouncements, despite the palpable sense of stalemate, and failed to provide any practical guidance for improving the situation. The chaotic withdrawal from Kabul in 2021, followed by a rapid return to Taliban rule, seemed to justify the cynicism that loomed over America's war. One soldier put the matter directly: 'Everything that we were told was bullshit.'[3]

The war in Afghanistan was, of course, part of a much larger response to the 11 September 2001 attacks. Afghanistan was the target of US military operations because the Taliban government provided support and sanctuary for the al-Qaeda terrorists who were responsible for the worst act of violence on the US in its history. The George W. Bush administration decided quickly to topple the Taliban and destroy al-Qaeda as a functioning organisation. But its counter-terrorism approach went much further. Because the administration believed that terrorist groups depended on state sponsorship, it started making plans for toppling other state sponsors. Efforts to prepare for a war in Iraq began soon after the fall of the Taliban in Afghanistan. The administration also launched a sweeping campaign against al-Qaeda and 'associated movements' operating in loose transnational networks. This campaign continues today, though in a somewhat modified form. Finally, the administration began a programme of public diplomacy designed to isolate extremist groups and make them less appealing to would-be recruits. The global war on terrorism would also constitute a war of ideas.[4]

The results were mixed. The Iraq war mirrored the experience in Afghanistan. Superior US military forces overwhelmed their rivals, toppled their regimes and set about the business of building friendlier new governments. Insurgent violence erupted in both countries, however, complicating US efforts. Overlapping ethnic, civil and sectarian wars made things much worse, as did the spread of organised crime and illicit economies. What had begun as an optimistic political exercise – a process of bringing fair laws, individual freedoms and representation to people long subject to authoritarian rule – descended into desperate efforts to maintain political stability amid gruesome bloodshed and thuggish opportunism. State-building was not a political experiment whose outcome was determined by debate and refinement, nor was it a peaceful competition to win the hearts and minds of civilians. It was a bloody contest for power.[5]

The quixotic effort to win civilian support in Afghanistan and Iraq foreshadowed the struggle to win the war of ideas. Observers offered a number of recommendations for public diplomacy in the immediate aftermath of the 9/11 attacks, given the urgent need to push back against al-Qaeda propaganda and repair America's image abroad. The Council on Foreign Relations, for instance, quickly convened a task force on the subject, and issued a series of organisational and substantive recommendations. This was critical, wrote the task force in its report, because 'if we are unable to win the battle for hearts and minds, it may prove impossible to carry our military operations through to completion'.[6] Success would make it hard for al-Qaeda to attract foot soldiers, financial backers or propagandists. Effective public diplomacy would also encourage international support for US counter-terrorism, making it easier for foreign leaders to cooperate with US efforts. International military, intelligence and law-enforcement coordination was necessary against transnational armed groups. It would be a lot easier to sustain coordination if global opinion remained sympathetic to the US cause.

Support for the US declined quickly, however. A Pew Research Center study in late 2003 found that international public opinion was deeply suspicious of the US, despite its efforts to invest in public diplomacy after 9/11. Opposition to the war in Iraq played a major role, but the Pew report emphasised deeper concerns about American 'power and policies'. US efforts to win the war of ideas proved to be marginal against these undercurrents.[7]

Big wars against terrorist state-sponsors were costly and divisive, and earnest efforts to win the war of ideas were disappointing. What remained were more direct actions against terrorists themselves. The US began an intensive effort to find terrorist groups, describe their capabilities and organisational structure, map their financing models and resource routes, and locate their personnel. It shared some of this information with international partners in joint counter-terrorism operations. In many cases the US acted unilaterally against those it identified as terrorists, using airstrikes and drone strikes. Special-operations forces came to play an outsize role in counter-terrorism, given their ability to move quickly and quietly against far-flung transnational groups with an interest in remaining hidden.

Open-ended counter-terrorism operations generated criticism, both foreign and domestic. Critics questioned the morality of lethal operations based on partial intelligence, especially 'signature strikes' that identified targets not through direct observation but through patterns of behaviour detected from distant surveillance platforms. The decision to use lethal force without positive identification of known terrorists raised the risk of killing or injuring civilians and made it difficult for the US to justify its actions as consistent with just-war principles.[8] Others warned that enthusiasm for counter-terrorism operations would backfire diplomatically. From this perspective, lethal operations conducted abroad reinforced the stereotype of America unrestrained and unconcerned about anyone else's sovereign rights.[9] And in the US, critics questioned the legal foundation of continued counter-terrorism strikes based on a congressional authorisation from nearly a quarter-century ago. When Congress authorised military force against al-Qaeda and the Taliban in 2001, critics asked, was this what it had in mind?[10]

Even those who support aggressive counter-terrorism expressed frustration. Victory has proven elusive, to the consternation of many observers, with significant consequences for military organisations, domestic politics and foreign policy. Continuous military action puts a real strain on resources and personnel. Close observers like Linda Robinson warned that 'US special forces face the serious danger of being bogged down in a permanent game of global whack-a-mole rather than operating as part of deliberate campaigns that can achieve lasting outcomes'.[11] Popular disillusionment with endless fighting might also contribute to a more general dissatisfaction with mainstream ideas about the United States' role in the world. According to one recent account, the constant drumbeat of counter-terrorism operations has been deeply divisive and has fuelled political tribalism at home.[12] The inability to declare victory, or at least bring the war to an honourable close, has energised critics of American counter-terrorism and frustrated its supporters.

*　*　*

Why does the US persist with an approach that seems so unsatisfying? There is probably no single answer, given the complex interplay between foreign policy, domestic politics, norms and law.[13] That said, the distinction between strategy and grand strategy goes a long way towards explaining one of the more puzzling aspects of contemporary US national security. Strategy tells a story about how states use military violence to achieve certain political objectives. If states cannot define those objectives, then strategy by definition is absurd. US officials always struggled to articulate the meaning of victory in the global war on terrorism. This is not because they were deliberately opaque, but because they were conducting a war among non-state groups operating on behalf of a loosely organised transnational movement.

Such a conflict does not lend itself to concrete measures of progress. Indeed, the war on terrorism never fit neatly into how we traditionally understand the use of force. Most wars end via coercion or conquest. Coercion occurs, per Carl von Clausewitz, when the winner compels the loser to do its will.[14] Military violence raises the cost of resistance, forcing states to recalculate the value of the political object against the price of continued fighting. If the price becomes prohibitive, they will sue for peace. In coercive wars, signs of the endgame range from private signals of distress to public calls for a settlement. Critically, however, the loser chooses when to quit. The British in the American War of Independence, for example, had the wherewithal to continue fighting for many years after Yorktown. But they chose to settle the conflict, calculating that the value of returning to the pre-war status quo did not justify the continued cost.

Wars of conquest are different. In contrast to wars of coercion, the goal is not settlement but subjugation, and the method is brute force. Conquest is appealing for rapacious states seeking new territories, as well as for states who have determined that their enemies are incorrigible. Because these wars are fundamentally tests of raw strength, the signs of impending victory are straightforward: industry destroyed, ground taken, enemy killed or captured and so on. There is less need to worry about political signals and peace overtures when the state is uninterested in a negotiated endgame. The Allies demanded unconditional surrender in the Second World War because the fascist powers were beyond negotiation, and indeed, beyond redemption. Only the destruction of their armed forces, military occupation and regime change would set the stage for a durable peace.

The goal in the global war on terrorism, however, is neither coercion nor conquest. Victory is not a matter of forcing enemies to surrender, because groups preaching martyrdom are beyond influencing. It may be possible to deter some of their supporters (e.g., financiers), just as it may be possible to deter some sympathisers from joining the cause.[15] But coercing leaders to abandon the fight is highly dubious, given their belief in an epic decades-long struggle requiring self-sacrifice. Indeed, some have argued that killing those leaders is necessary to have any influence over terrorist groups.[16] Terrorism researchers have argued that deterrence is possible in some circumstances, but this is not the same as compelling a surrender.

Nor is the goal destroying their ability to resist. The US and its partners attacked al-Qaeda's capabilities after 9/11, of course. They killed and captured most of the group's original leaders; they destroyed former training camps; and they worked to starve the group of financial resources.[17] US special-operations forces developed counter-network tactics that were highly effective in Iraq and Afghanistan, and their targeting doctrine expanded to other theatres.[18] This algorithmic approach constituted a form of institutionalised manhunting, and it worked. US forces rightfully claimed tactical successes against the original al-Qaeda and several regional offshoots.

The offshoots, however, are the problem. Unlike nation-states, al-Qaeda and most of its ideological brethren do not require territorial control or the trappings of bureaucracy.[19] Physical damage is costly but not conclusive. What matters is their reputation for resistance: the movement claims to be a bulwark against Western political and cultural expansion. This image is surely appealing to like-minded militants in other countries, and there is nothing stopping them from adopting the symbols and ethos of the original al-Qaeda. Brute-force attacks on key organisations are effective in the near term but strategically indecisive, especially if they leave a trail of martyrs behind. Anyone can pick up the mantle of resistance; anyone can claim a regional franchise.

Successful counter-terrorism after 9/11 was not a matter of coercion or conquest. Instead, it was a matter of risk acceptance. The question was not how to force terrorists to surrender, or what it would take to destroy their capabilities, but whether political leaders were willing to bear the risk of subsequent attacks if they removed military personnel from active theatres. This was (and is) a difficult and subjective test. Keeping forces deployed abroad for extended periods invites military atrophy and public disillusionment. Bringing those forces home too soon risks a backlash if terrorist groups reconstitute their organisational strength and go on the offensive. There is no obvious way of locating the culminating point of counter-terrorism, the moment at which it makes sense to wind down operations.[20]

President Barack Obama faced this dilemma in his approach to the war in Iraq. Obama was famously critical of the decision to invade. Unlike then-senator Hillary Clinton, he opposed the war in 2003, and his vocal stance helped distinguish Obama from his future rival for the Democratic presidential nomination in 2008. As a candidate, he argued that Iraq pulled American attention from more pressing security threats. Intervening in Afghanistan was a sensible response to the 9/11 attacks, and US forces ought to have focused their efforts on hunting for Osama bin Laden and destroying al-Qaeda once and for all. As president, Obama made good on his promise to withdraw from Iraq, ordering a military exit in 2011. Yet the rapid offensive of the self-styled Islamic State (ISIS) in 2014 put pressure on the White House to reverse that decision. Compared to other militant groups, ISIS seemed unusually capable and well organised. But what made it particularly alarming was its embrace of shocking and grisly violence, which it publicised widely on social media. The group was a nightmare: a terrifying blend of competence and depravity. Pressure to respond quickly mounted in Washington, lest it expand its violent campaign against American targets. Obama relented to this pressure in the summer of 2013, returning US forces to Iraq, where they remain as of late 2024.

President Joe Biden faced a similar dilemma. After his election in 2020, he quickly set about withdrawing US forces from Afghanistan, pledging to end a war that had become deeply frustrating. Like Obama a decade earlier, he followed through, ordering a US exit in his first year in office. For Biden, the status quo was no longer acceptable. 'Already we have members of our military whose parents fought in Afghanistan 20 years ago', he declared, channelling a sense of national disillusionment with a seemingly endless war. 'Would you send their children and their grandchildren as well? Would you send your own son or daughter?'[21] Better, from his perspective, to bring them home. The US would largely end its military and political commitment to Afghanistan. Efforts to rebuild Afghanistan's government and economy had reached the point of declining marginal returns; Afghanistan's leaders and people needed to take responsibility for their own future. Meanwhile, US forces would adopt a different approach to counter-terrorism that relied on offshore surveillance:

> Our military and intelligence leaders are confident they have the capabilities to protect the homeland and our interests from any resurgent terrorist challenge emerging or emanating from Afghanistan. We are developing a counter-terrorism over-the-horizon capability that will allow us to keep our eyes firmly fixed on any direct threats to the United States in the region, and act quickly and decisively if needed.[22]

Not everyone was reassured. Critics warned that the US withdrawal increased the danger that Afghanistan would once again become a hub for terrorist violence, inexorably pulling the US back to the region. As one former senior Pentagon official put it: 'A peace that deserts our allies and enables our enemies to seize power will raise the risks of renewed terrorist attacks on the American homeland … Such an outcome might draw us back into future military operations in the region on far more disadvantageous terms.'[23] Biden did not yield to this pressure and appeared convinced that the over-the-horizon military posture was working.

Yet even Biden, whose instincts were more cautious and restrained than those of his predecessors, did not halt counter-terrorism operations. As of this writing, US forces continue to operate across wide swathes of Asia and Africa. Biden's concerns about the open-ended war in Afghanistan apparently did not apply to the broader war on terrorism, despite the fact that military force seemed disconnected from political goals. Indeed, it is not clear that these operations are linked to political goals at all. For this reason, strategy does not provide much analytical traction for those seeking to understand counter-terrorism in Afghanistan, Iraq and elsewhere. Grand strategy, however, might help.

*   *   *

The goal of grand strategy is security, not victory. It is about gaining a sense of safety, not achieving some tangible political objective. As a result, military operations may contribute to security even if they are logically removed from practical policy objectives. They will not lead to an 'end state' because there is no end to the search for security.[24] Instead, they serve to keep threats in check at a reasonable cost. What constitutes meaningful threats and reasonable costs are subjective questions, which is why debates over grand strategy are interminable.

The logic of grand strategy explains why the US stayed in Afghanistan for so long, despite widespread public disillusionment. Efforts to build a self-sustaining government in Kabul foundered, as did efforts to compel the revived Taliban to stop fighting. At the same time, however, US forces learned to use the country as a base of operations against terrorist groups while reducing the costs. The Taliban thrived in sparsely populated rural areas but struggled to make headway in cities, producing a rough military balance for the last several years of the war. US casualties were also very low during that time. Eleven servicemembers were killed in hostile action in 2017; 13 in 2018; 17 in 2019; and four in 2020.[25] Advocates of an enduring American ground presence in Afghanistan argued that the counterterrorism gains justified these losses. Until 2021, they were able to convince sceptical policymakers to go along.[26]

The broader war on terrorism also makes sense in terms of grand strategy, not strategy, especially when considered in the post-Cold War context. Policymakers from both parties embraced the idea that the world is safer when there is a single dominant power. The existence of a hegemon promoted security, stability and prosperity. In this respect the US acted, as former secretary of state Madeleine Albright put it, as 'the indispensable nation'.[27] The hegemon facilitated international cooperation by resolving collective-action problems. It provided an economic safety net by coordinating international action during times of crisis and offering a currency of last resort. Most importantly, it prevented war by deterring challengers to the international order and putting down those who might be foolish enough to try.

This last point is key to understanding why US leaders have continued to operate against scattered terrorists around the world. Groups like al-Qaeda explicitly proclaim their opposition to the US and the international order it has built in its image. Concerns for its reputation have impelled Washington to respond forcefully to such groups, despite the fact that they are comparatively tiny. Walking away from such threats, according to this logic, would damage US credibility, undermining international confidence in the US-led order.

The purpose of grand strategy is security, a subjective condition informed by psychology and politics as much as the objective balance of power. A state may feel insecure even if it achieves wartime victory. Conversely, the experience of losing may cause the state to feel more secure over the long term if the experience inspires overdue institutional reforms. And unlike victory in war, security is not time-bound. States do not feel permanently secure, no matter their current advantages. Leaders of unusually strong states look warily upon much smaller adversaries, sensing that they cannot be truly safe unless they remain vigilant. Leaders who espouse a grand strategy of primacy are particularly prone to this sort of threat inflation. The relentless pursuit of security as such encourages it.

Critics of grand strategy, however, warn that this pursuit is subject to abuse.[28] A theory of security may be conceptually clear, but measuring progress is difficult because of the subjective nature of 'security'. How to define security, and how to decide how much is enough, are ultimately political judgements. Such questions do not lend themselves to quantification, and they are rarely answered to everyone's satisfaction. Ironically, however, the same properties of grand strategy that make the concept so aggravating, also allow it to accommodate ambiguous military campaigns.

Late imperial Britain provides a useful illustration.[29] In the aftermath of the First World War, the cash-strapped empire sought a way to patrol far-flung territories without deploying too many personnel abroad, and without sacrificing resources needed for homeland defence. Instead of maintaining large garrisons in Africa, the Middle East and Asia, enthusiastic airmen convinced the government that routine bombing could quell rebellions and help to maintain British control. Airpower, they believed, would eliminate key rebel leaders, drive foot soldiers into hiding and deter civilians from joining any kind of insurgency. They called it 'air policing'.[30]

British air forces began in 1919 by bombing targets in Afghanistan. The campaign did not do much physical damage, but officials in the Air Ministry believed it had significant coercive effects. The British took this concept to Africa in January 1920, using bombing raids to kill leaders of a rebellion in British Somaliland who had resisted four previous ground offensives. Energised by the apparent success of air policing, a seemingly cheap and easy alternative to ground power, the British soon expanded the programme to Iraq and other imperial holdings.[31] Airpower advocates made their case before members of Parliament, who were receptive given the reality of tight budgets and the memory of grinding land warfare in the First World War.[32]

Air policing was not quite the same as war. There was no logical expiration date for operations; British leaders assumed that occasional insurgencies were inevitable, much as city leaders assume some level of crime. The government was under no illusion that raids would lead to a durable political settlement with rebels, or that bombing would permanently end the problem of rebellion. Instead, bombing was a low-cost tactic for maintaining control, while enabling local allies who provided boots on the ground.

The US approach to terrorism is similar. Even before the 9/11 attacks, US officials had become dubious of large-footprint military campaigns, and hoped to use new technologies that would allow them to fight with fewer numbers.[33] The use of airpower, if it works as an independent tool, greatly reduces the strain on personnel who would otherwise be subject to repeated and lengthy deployments.[34] Precision bombing holds out the promise of eliminating terrorist leaders, disrupting their networks and making it difficult for them to gather and organise attacks. Drones are particularly useful because they are inexpensive, plentiful, disposable and able to loiter over targets for much longer than crewed aircraft.

Most importantly, US efforts will not end terrorism any more than the British believed they could eliminate rebellion. Counter-terrorist operations, no matter how effective, cannot prevent individuals from joining non-state armed groups or participating in violence. At best they can manage the problem by degrading terrorist groups and by deterring some individuals from joining in the first place. These results can increase security even though they cannot deliver victory. Put another way, the US version of air policing is comprehensible in terms of grand strategy but makes little sense in terms of strategy.

The analogy is far from perfect. British air policing relied heavily on the idea that bombs would terrorise civilians. The US, by contrast, has tried to reduce the threat to civilians, though critics argue it hasn't done enough.[35] That said, the British experience remains a useful comparison. Like the current effort, air policing appealed to budget-conscious legislators who sought to exploit innovative weapons in favour of raw manpower. Aircraft technology was still new when it appeared in the interwar period, just as drones were relatively rare at the start of the global war on terrorism. The asymmetric advantage arguably helped both states deal with particularly dangerous organisations, even if it could not deliver comprehensive results. Making the most of airpower, whether in the form of canvas-winged biplanes or high-altitude drones, depends on local intelligence about insurgent groups and their leaders. Gaining that knowledge created new risks for local partners. Yet for Britain and the US, the political costs were manageable.

Imperial air policing ended when Britain could no longer afford an empire. Whatever costs it saved through bombing were overwhelmed by two world wars and a series of post-war economic disasters. The US is likely to continue for longer, given that it has a much larger financial buffer.[36] And although counter-terrorism has produced a great deal of angst, it is a relatively minor issue for most voters. Public opinion soured on the wars in Afghanistan and Iraq, where US forces established a large ground footprint, but there is little sustained domestic opposition to a strategy focused mainly on intelligence, special operations and drone strikes.[37] As long as there are no serious economic or political pressures to exercise restraint, we can expect more of the same: an imperial-style policing campaign waged by a country without an imperial constabulary.

\* \* \*

Distinguishing between strategy and grand strategy helps resolve two related puzzles. It explains why the US spent so long fighting an intractable war in Afghanistan, and why it continues to pursue a war on terrorism without a clear definition of victory. In terms of strategy, the conflicts are nonsensical. The American approach only comes into focus through the lens of grand strategy. This argument says nothing about the quality of US military operations; my purpose is not to judge them one way or the other. Indeed, both supporters and critics can use the logic above to develop their arguments. Supporters believe that an indefinite forward presence coupled with aggressive counter-terrorist operations is necessary to keep security threats at a manageable level, and they emphasise the relatively low costs in blood and treasure. Critics argue that such operations are potentially counterproductive if they contribute to anti-American sentiment, and that the long-term costs are substantial. From their perspective, an open-ended approach to counter-terrorism will strain US diplomacy, stretch US military forces and corrode US politics.

US grand-strategic interests have evolved since the most intense phase of the war on terrorism, of course. Deteriorating relations with Russia and China have led the Department of Defense to refocus on great-power competition, and it has deemed China the 'pacing challenge' around which it plans. Although counter-terrorism operations continue apace, three consecutive administrations have signalled their desire to concentrate more of their resources on East Asian security. This creates a host of familiar challenges for strategy and grand strategy, some of which I discussed in the last chapter. The problem of nuclear escalation looms large in a hypothetical US–China conflict and it is not surprising that analysts have returned to the debate over the theory of the nuclear revolution. Washington and Beijing are both in the process of modernising their nuclear forces, leading to a debate among observers about their underlying purposes. Is the US simply trying to bring legacy systems up to date, or is it trying to develop the capability to pull off a first strike? Is China attempting to restore deterrence by developing its capability for assured retaliation, or does it believe that it can use a stronger nuclear force to deter US entry into a regional war?

China and the US clearly believe that nuclear weapons play a key role in grand strategy, whether their theory of security is ambitious or restrained. Less clear is whether they would actually cross the nuclear threshold in a conflict. If the theory of the nuclear revolution is correct, then they will back away from the brink, just like their great-power predecessors did in the Cold War. If not, then a US–China conflict might escalate unpredictably with enormous consequences. No one knows whether the US will intervene in the defence of regional allies and partners, or whether China will risk catastrophe to enforce its territorial claims. Moreover, some analysts fear that the grand-strategic use of nuclear weapons (e.g., for deterrence) might raise the risk of inadvertent escalation in a deep crisis. Overconfidence about nuclear signalling in peacetime might lead to nuclear disaster in war.

Other factors complicate a potential conflict. One is that a US–China clash would represent the first great-power war fought between sophisticated cyberspace actors. Military doctrine in both countries emphasises the importance of information superiority, and both countries have invested heavily in defensive and offensive cyberspace capabilities. The implication is that much of the strategic interaction in war will occur in a radically different war-fighting domain. But while ideas about 'cyber war' seem exotic, such a conflict would not be the first time that great powers pondered the problem of operating in previously inaccessible spaces. In the Renaissance, emerging naval technologies allowed strategists to theorise about the nature of war on blue water. In the twentieth century, emerging aircraft technologies allowed strategists to imagine victory through airpower. In both cases, as we will see in the next chapter, strategists were simultaneously enthralled with and fearful about the possibilities of operating in a new domain. These innovations also provoked important questions about grand strategy, and they encouraged new thinking about the underlying sources of national security. How will cyberspace and related innovations affect strategy and grand strategy today? What can we learn from past cases? What are the implications for the US–China military balance? And what are the implications for war?

## CHAPTER FIVE

# Strategy, grand strategy and emerging technologies

Americans have high hopes for new tech. Appeals to techno-logical solutions for strategic problems have a long history in the United States; recent breakthroughs in cyberspace and artificial intelligence (AI) have inspired visions of future wars fought quickly and decisively.[1] In an important sense, those visions represent an evolution of the American way of war for the last three decades. Since the end of the Cold War, the US military has followed an operational script that exploits tech-nological advantages to fight and win quickly. Blinding strikes against intelligence and command-and-control systems leave the enemy unable to organise a coherent defence, allowing US forces to control the scope and pace of fighting. Although this logic was originally associated with airpower, operations in cyberspace are naturally suited to such an approach, and the long-standing US lead in computer science and adjacent disci-plines suggests that future innovations will allow it to indulge its war-fighting preferences. It is no surprise that defence offi-cials have embraced the digital domain.[2]

At the same time, they worry that China will use cyber-space in novel ways to overcome its material disadvantages in a future war. Defence officials are particularly concerned about Beijing's interest in 'cognitive warfare', a concept that 'combines psychological warfare with cyber operations to shape adversary behaviour and decision making'.[3] This approach targets US perceptions before a conflict and may seek to undermine its sense of common purpose after the shooting starts. According to the Pentagon's 2023 annual report on Chinese capabilities, the People's Liberation Army (PLA) 'probably intends to use [cognitive domain operations] as an asymmetric capability to deter US or third-party entry into a future conflict, or as an offensive capability to shape perceptions or polarize a society'.[4]

These hopes and fears are especially intense when it comes to AI. In theory, AI-enabled platforms will support extremely rapid information processing and battlefield awareness, giving a clear advantage to armies that learn to harness AI for military purposes. Intelligence services will provide early warning of enemy intentions; military commanders will lean on AI decision aids to optimise their strategic choices; and fielded forces will be able to detect enemy movements and direct responses. Because war is now moving too fast for human beings, military organisations that cannot use AI effectively will risk rapid defeat. Air Force Lieutenant-General Jack Shanahan, the inaugural commander of the Pentagon's Joint Artificial Intelligence Center, hinted at the future wartime consequences of falling behind. 'What I don't want to see', he said, 'is a future where our potential adversaries have a fully AI-enabled force and we do not'.[5]

The balance of grand strategy, we are told, is also on the line. According to the congressionally mandated National Security Commission on Artificial Intelligence, leadership in AI technologies confers massive advantages because of the vast number of military and economic applications. American grand strategy has usually benefited from its scientific and engineering base, allowing it to develop and deploy new technologies faster than its great-power rivals. That may not be the case today. Indeed, the Commission warns that China is seizing the opportunity to leapfrog the US, despite the legacy of past American innovations, with grave consequences for American security and prosperity. 'China possesses the might, talent, and ambition to surpass the United States as the world's leader in AI in the next decade if current trends do not change.'[6]

Advances in space technology, meanwhile, have encouraged planners to imagine complex earthbound operations overseen and coordinated from orbiting platforms. US interest in exploiting space for war-fighting purposes dates to the early Cold War, though technical difficulties kept US forces from achieving some of their wildest aspirations.[7] Futurists may have envisioned space as a battlefield, but the physics of space travel and the limits of contemporaneous technology made these visions impractical. Instead of fighting in space, it learned how to use space to fight more effectively on Earth. Beginning in the 1960s, the US fielded a constellation of communications and intelligence satellites. These in turn provided the foundation for remarkable advances in geolocation and precision, which allowed US commanders to target enemy forces while reducing the risk of fratricide or civilian harm. Some enthusiasts believed that they were fundamental to the technological revolution that was 'lifting the fog of war'.[8]

American grand strategy also relies on space superiority. Unfettered access to space provides early warning and allows the intelligence community to monitor distant places without provoking political crises.[9] Sharing imagery and other forms of space-based intelligence is also a potentially important diplomatic tool, strengthening US alliances and partnerships, and bolstering arms-control treaties.[10] Finally, it has become essential to peacetime conventional power projection.

US grand strategy relies on the assumption that it can rapidly move forces across long distances and coordinate military action in multiple domains. None of this would be possible without a reliable space-based communications infrastructure.[11]

Unsurprisingly, the increasing value of space has led to growing fears about anti-satellite (ASAT) weapons. Reliance on a relatively small number of space assets implied a serious wartime risk, because reasonably capable adversaries would surely try to take them out. Cold War defence officials were highly sensitive to intelligence on Soviet ASAT programmes. Their fears resurfaced after China's ASAT test in 2007, when Beijing successfully destroyed a decrepit satellite in low-earth orbit. More recently, US officials have warned that Russia may seek to use nuclear weapons against satellites. Such a decision would cross two Rubicons at once: the first use of nuclear weapons since Hiroshima and Nagasaki, and the transformation of space into a war-fighting domain.[12]

Although it is harder to discern Chinese perceptions, the view from Beijing reflects a similar mix of hope and fear about emerging technologies. Chinese military doctrine emphasises the importance of controlling information in war, for example, especially in early stages of a conflict. Modern military operations depend on reliable communications, and the geography of maritime East Asia puts a premium on the ability to coordinate ground, air and naval forces. Attacks on rival information systems thus offer a neat way of seizing the initiative and unsettling their efforts to organise a response. The 2001 edition of the Science of Military Strategy, a highly influential statement published by the PLA, states that precision strikes at the outset of war could 'paralyze the enemy in one stroke'. A recent update to the strategy focuses on the 'effective suppression and destruction' of an enemy's information systems alongside an 'information protection capability'.

Chinese leaders believe that they cannot win if they cannot 'seize and control the battlefield initiative, paralyze and destroy the enemy's operational system of systems, and shock the enemy's will for war'.[13]

Chinese investment in AI is consistent with its belief in taking the initiative and controlling information in a conflict. Despite the recent experience of the US and Russia, both of whom expected short wars and found themselves stuck in long ones, Chinese doctrine continues to emphasise the importance of the first exchange. Speed is particularly important in a hypothetical conflict with the US, because early Chinese operational gains would put Washington on the horns of a dilemma. Any decision to go to war in East Asia will be difficult, given the costs and risks. But going in after a successful Chinese attack on American bases and communications will be especially fraught because it will be much harder to reconstitute forces and to organise a surge into China's maritime backyard. Pulling off such a coup will not be easy for the PLA, however, given the simple fact that the US possesses the most technologically advanced military in the world. Beating US forces to the punch will require exquisite knowledge of US capabilities, and the ability to make rapid early-war decisions about how to attack them. AI-enabled intelligence and decision aids are probably attractive to Chinese military planners for these reasons. More broadly, Chinese leaders seem to share the US belief that superiority in AI will have meaningful effects on the material balance of power, and its grand strategy follows the presumption that technological progress is foundational to bolstering its national security. The Chinese Communist Party, the PLA and China's commercial leaders have placed big bets on AI.[14]

China is also betting on space. In 2002, then-Communist Party general secretary Jiang Zemin described space as 'the new strategic high ground of international military competition', and directed new investments in ASAT weapons. Jiang noted that the US had used satellite capabilities effectively in Iraq, Kosovo and Afghanistan, and argued that counter-space capabilities would be useful for interrupting US conventional military operations. Counter-space assets were particularly appealing to China, because the Americans seemed increasingly dependent on a small number of vulnerable platforms in fixed orbits. Attacking those platforms held out the promise of hobbling US efforts to coordinate the activities of forces in a vast maritime theatre; perhaps the ASAT threat would be enough to deter Washington from intervening in the first place. Two years later, however, his successor Hu Jintao remarked that China faced a 'five-dimensional battlefield' that included a 'space battlefield', warning that China's adversaries were rushing to improve their capabilities in orbit. China had a rational interest in exploiting space to deter or defeat US forces, but it also had a reasonable fear that it would be overwhelmed in an arms race. Failure to stop the US from deploying a secure constellation of space assets suggested an indefinite period of earthbound military inferiority.[15]

Contemporary debates about strategy and grand strategy are obsessed with technology. Exotic innovations in cyber-space, AI and space have triggered a new look at old ideas. This is not the first time that great powers have grappled with the implications of technological breakthroughs, however. Critical scientific and engineering milestones have prompted fundamental reconsideration about the best way to fight and win wars – and the best way to secure the state in peacetime. How did states alter their views in the aftermath of innovation? How did the experience affect strategy and grand strategy? Is there a pattern that emerges across time and space? And if so, what are the implications for US–China rivalry today? This chapter pursues these questions, with a specific focus on cyberspace.

## Hope, fear and resignation

Emerging technologies provoke new questions about strategy and grand strategy. What happens, for example, when peacetime innovation opens up new war-fighting domains?[16] Technological breakthroughs sometimes make it possible to operate in previously inaccessible places. The advent of large sailing vessels in the sixteenth century suggested the possibility of naval action far from shore. This had implications for grand strategy, as it made naval imperialism a possibility for any state with the money and infrastructure to maintain a blue-water fleet. It also opened new possibilities for victory in war through naval power. Fleet-on-fleet battles might prove decisive if the victor could control sea lines of commerce and threaten the enemy's economic survival. The advent of strategic bombers led to quite similar discussions in the twentieth century. Some observers argued that bomber superiority was essential for national security because bombers could fly over front lines and target enemy cities directly. Maintaining a strong bomber fleet was thus a deterrent against enemy aggression and, they hoped, a source of enduring peace. Should deterrence break down, future wars would be decided quickly: whichever bomber fleet managed to survive the first volley would have unfettered control for the rest of the conflict. Bomber supremacy, like naval supremacy, would confer enormous leverage over enemies during war and in the aftermath.

Post-war breakthroughs in rocketry and satellite technologies led to similar hopes about space control. Mastering space physics and engineering would make it possible to vastly improve intelligence-gathering against enemies and coordinate terrestrial forces. Improved ballistic missiles could move through space unobstructed and impervious to defences on the ground. Controlling the 'ultimate high ground' was seductive to observers who envisioned future fighting as something utterly different from the grinding industrial world wars of the twentieth century.

Hopes that emerging technologies would transform strategy and grand strategy existed alongside fears that other states would get there first. If it was possible to build a naval fleet that could win wars quickly and decisively, then losing quickly and decisively was also possible. The same fears rang true during the intense strategic-bombing debate in the interwar years. Failure to build large bombers en masse and create independent air forces, warned bomber advocates, would leave the state disastrously vulnerable. Inferiority would mean peacetime helplessness and wartime disaster.

Such dreams and nightmares never materialised. Technologies in new domains had important impacts on war and peace, to be sure, but hopes of rapid victory were dashed by practical and political limitations. Choreographing large naval battles proved extraordinarily difficult: finding an enemy fleet and keeping it fixed in place were often impossible. Moreover, enemy economies proved adaptable and resilient even in the face of naval blockade and coastal bombardment. The same was true for bombers, who struggled mightily in the Second World War to find and demolish important targets. The victims of bombing, moreover, found workarounds to keep producing war materials, and civilians were as likely to demand revenge as they were to demand a settlement in the wake of bombing raids. Space proved most difficult of all. The practical expense and staggering complexity of space operations were barriers to entry for almost everyone. Even the superpowers struggled. While they achieved important breakthroughs, especially in communications and intelligence, the idea of actually fighting in space remained in the realm of science fiction. International agreements to prohibit the weaponisation of space were diplomatically straightforward in spirit, though US and Soviet negotiators could not come to an agreement on a standard definition of a 'space weapon', and in any case few believed that it was technologically feasible.[17] Translating control of a new domain into strategic results was never straightforward.

Nor were these innovations the key to post-war dominance. Mastery of technologies that enabled combat in new domains did not mean mastery over the domain itself. States did not sit idly as a first mover deployed revolutionary capabilities. Instead, they developed their own offensive and defensive capabilities so that they too could operate in new spaces. And if they were unable to keep up, they found ways to mitigate the consequences. Land powers, for instance, learned to deal with superior navies by improving land-borne transportation networks for domestic and regional commerce. They also found ways to combat maritime economic coercion. Smuggling helped, as did efforts to support rebellions against naval empires with limited resources for controlling land. Technological superiority was important for great powers, to be sure, but it did not guarantee political inferiority for their rivals.

States did not gain enduring strategic or grand-strategic benefits from moving rapidly into new war-fighting domains. Those who had dreamed of dominance were disappointed. Those who had worried about subservience were relieved. What actually transpired was interesting, though much less dramatic. Periods of innovation inspired a sequence of hope, fear and resignation. States hoped that they could build new war-fighting tools that would ensure victory over their rivals in new domains, and that they could turn those victories into lasting political gains. They soon realised, however, that they might come out on the wrong side if their rivals made better investments and learned how to operate more effectively. The fear of late arrival was the black mirror to rosy visions of power and prosperity delivered by new technologies in new domains.

Over time, however, states settled into a kind of resignation about the limits of military operations on blue water, in the sky and in space. Practical and political issues dampened early enthusiasm for the possibilities of fighting in new domains and alleviated early fears. States did not stop their work, of course, but they lowered their expectations.

Defence officials describe cyberspace as the newest war-fighting domain, and military organisations have developed sophisticated tools for targeting adversary information systems. Will their efforts trigger the familiar pattern of hope, fear and resignation? Or is the domain fundamentally different in ways that foreshadow something else entirely? Does the evidence from the Russia–Ukraine war, the first major conflict among sophisticated cyber powers, shed any light on the question? And what can we say about the possible effects of cyberspace operations in a hypothetical war between the US and China?

## Strategy and grand strategy in cyberspace

Cyberspace is different. It is entirely artificial, a sprawling communications and data-storage architecture built and maintained by human beings. For this reason, not everyone agrees that it should count as a war-fighting domain like the sea or the sky. Characterising cyberspace this way may have helped explain it to military officers, but it is analytically misleading.[18] Nor is it clear that 'war' is the right way to describe cyberspace competition. Writing just after the Cold War, prominent analysts claimed that wars were becoming contests over information control, not bloody battles of attrition and manoeuvre.[19] Sceptics disagreed, arguing that it made little sense to refer to non-violent information battles as wars. Cyberspace operations might enable war fighting, but they could not logically replace it.[20]

Whatever the merits of these arguments, military services are investing heavily, perhaps because they see possibilities for quick, decisive victory. Well-executed cyberspace operations might force enemies into operational sclerosis by corrupting communications. This scenario is especially appealing today, given the complexity of war plans that require tight integration among sea, air and land forces. Disrupting information is likely to disrupt enemy battlefield effectiveness. It is not hard to understand the appeal of cyberspace to strategists and operational planners.[21]

Like the other domains, cyberspace also arouses fear of rapid defeat. Enemy attacks evoke nightmares of blank screens, lost ships and inoperable systems. Even less dramatic attacks might impact military performance, given the degree to which modern militaries rely on information technology. Advanced communications have allowed states to monitor the battlefield, coordinate activities among disparate units and share granular information in near-real time. Losing trust in those communications' technology – because the data is either unavailable or corrupted – might cause them to revert to an old-fashioned and costly approach to fighting.[22] In addition, some fear that enemies will use cyberspace as a vector for propaganda and misinformation. The peculiar attributes of social media create an environment in which false information can spread quickly and easily. War has always included a large dose of deception; cyberspace might make the problem much more complex and daunting. Most recently, national-security officials have speculated that states will use malware against civilian infrastructure to inspire confusion and panic.[23]

States have responded to these dangers. Many have built large military organisations dedicated to offensive and defensive cyberspace operations.[24] US military cyberspace grew from modest origins to a unified combatant command, and some observers are calling for a sixth service entirely devoted to the digital domain, complementing the US Army, Navy,

Air Force, Marine Corps and Space Force.[25] Yet bureaucratic expansion creates problems of its own. Critics note that the traditional measures of military effectiveness make little sense in cyberspace, meaning that military officers might struggle to define what they mean by success. They also wonder if rigid military hierarchies can succeed in the first place, given the irreverent culture that characterises the private-sector hacker community.[26]

A deeper problem is that cyberspace is fickle. Users, firms, states and international governing bodies constantly renegotiate the protocols that enable data transfer, with important effects on the possibility and limits of cyberspace operations.[27] The increasingly blurred line between the digital and physical worlds makes it hard to distinguish one domain from the other, or to make confident predictions about the utility of cyber attacks in future conflicts.[28] Optimising institutional performance is easier when tasks are well structured and unchanging, but this is not the case here.[29] Similarly, the effectiveness of cyber attacks depends on the ability to exploit accesses to rival information networks. These accesses are prone to disappear, sometimes because of aggressive counter-intelligence activities and sometimes for prosaic reasons like routine software updates.[30] Cyber attacks are not 'target agnostic' because malware exploits specific vulnerabilities and military forces cannot hold targets at risk the way they do in the physical world.[31]

The technical realties of cyberspace have led some analysts to ratchet down their expectations for what they might achieve in wartime. Hopes for 'information dominance' are likely to prove disappointing.[32] Instead of planning for offensive cyberspace operations that have extraordinary effects, analysts have spent more time recently discussing how to operate conventional forces in partially degraded environments.[33]

In this sense, attitudes about cyberspace echo the pattern of hope, fear and resignation that we have witnessed in other new domains. Early hopes of exploiting cyberspace operations to achieve decisive results gave rise to fear of catastrophic defeat. Over time, however, observers realised that technical and organisational problems stood in the way. Strategists stopped thinking about using new instruments as independent war-winning tools and more so as complements for existing capabilities.

That said, it is possible that war will be the real test of cyber capabilities. Political leaders are still advocating for more investment in cyber capabilities, and military and intelligence leaders are sounding the alarm about malicious cyberspace actors. A recent congressional committee, which I discuss in more detail below, focused on the threat of Chinese intrusions into US infrastructure. Intelligence, law-enforcement and homeland-security leaders voiced ominous warnings about the effects of potential Chinese operations in war. Their comments suggest that hope and fear have not yet given way to resignation.

\* \* \*

In peacetime, states have mixed grand-strategic incentives because cyberspace is a multi-use domain: the same information networks are used for intelligence collection, strategic communications, military coordination and economic exchange.[34] The US extols a liberal approach to cyberspace as a venue for commerce and conversation, yet it has reportedly used cyberspace for offensive purposes. Critics warn that such activities may cause states, firms and users to become less enthusiastic about the domain. If their warnings are right, then the parochial benefits of offensive action may undermine the long-term national interest.

The trade-off will be particularly acute in the event of a military conflict, given the pressing demands of war. States may be willing to use cyberspace tools without taking steps to mitigate the risk of damaging third-party networks and machines. The effects of widespread data corruption and undiscovered malware may linger long after the war's end. In this scenario, wartime cyberspace operations may undermine the value of the domain later. Strategy will work against grand strategy.

How states weigh these trade-offs depends on their beliefs about grand strategy. If states are committed to rebuilding a liberal international order following the rise of a number of illiberal regimes, then they may decide to err on the side of caution and avoid the temptation to use offensive cyberspace operations for parochial gain. A genuine commitment to liberal values would require considerable restraint. Their calculations also depend on their beliefs about the nature of the domain. If states believe that cyberspace is resilient, then they will increase their activities. If they worry that cyberspace is fragile, then they will be cautious.[35]

The foundation of post-Cold War US grand strategy has been overwhelming material strength. Economic and military dominance has enabled an ambitious theory of security: the US has worked very hard to expand its vision for global order and sustain its position at the top. Some defence officials worry, however, that weaker adversaries will erode US strength through routine harassment rather than challenging it directly. Cyberspace is a good place to impose costs on the US, given the abundance of non-state proxies and the ability to target all elements of US society. Pinprick cyberspace operations will not provoke a military response and, these officials fear, the authors can disclaim responsibility anyway. The effects of these attacks will accumulate over time, officials warn, in ways that put a dent in the US lead.[36]

Over the last decade the US has become more assertive in cyber-space. In 2018 the Department of Defense declared its intention to 'defend forward' and mitigate threats as close as possible to their point of origin. US Cyber Command operationalised this guidance through what it calls 'persistent engagement', an approach which stresses the need for vigilance in a domain of continuous interac-tion with malicious actors.[37] US policy and doctrine statements do not assume that adversaries will become less aggressive over time as a result of US activism. In fact, it assumes the opposite. The resulting approach is thus more aggressive about confronting adversaries in cyberspace, but less ambitious about trying to influ-ence their behaviour.

Although the notion of cumulative effects is concerning, in an important sense it reflects a less ominous vision of grand strategy in the cyber era. The problem is not about digital disasters, the nightmares about a 'cyber Pearl Harbor' that would throw the US economy into chaos. Indeed, the shift from worrying about catastrophe to worrying about long-term erosion represents a somewhat sanguine view of the dangers of cyber attacks. Policymakers may have wondered why there had not been a significant event, despite the apparent vulnerability of US networks. Perhaps they had exaggerated those vulnerabilities. Or perhaps they had given US adversaries too much credit. It is not easy to engineer an electronic attack that even remotely approaches the death and destruction caused by natural disasters.[38] Whatever the reason, it seemed that policymakers were settling into a period of resignation about the consequences of cyberspace operations for US grand strategy.

Recent rhetoric, however, suggests an official return to older fears. In 2020, the Congressional Cyberspace Solarium Commission painted a grim picture of Washington in the after-math of a cyberspace attack. And in early 2024, Cybersecurity and Infrastructure Security Agency (CISA) Director Jen Easterly offered a particularly dire scenario in congressional testimony: 'Telecommunications going down – People start getting sick from polluted water. Trains get derailed. This is truly an everything, everywhere, all at once scenario.'[39] It seems that not all leaders are resigned to a vision of cyberspace in which damage accumulates slowly. Instead, comments like Easterly's suggest a return to treating cyberspace operations as weapons of mass destruction.

What might this rhetorical shift mean for grand strategy? If it is a temporary aberration, then we may see Washington continue the pattern of hope, fear and resignation. But as of this writing, officials do not sound like they are resigned to anything, and if they return to viewing cyberspace operations as akin to nuclear weapons, then we will probably see more serious efforts to restore deterrence to the digital domain. Meanwhile critics will intensify their calls for restraint, much as Cold War critics urged leaders not to send unnecessarily provocative nuclear signals. Hawks and doves may unite in their assumptions about the danger of large-scale attacks, even if they disagree about what to do about it. In this case the familiar grand-strategy debate among those favouring more or less activism will be replicated in debates over cyberspace policy.

### The Russia–Ukraine war

Evidence from Russia's invasion of Ukraine might shed light on strategy and grand strategy in cyberspace. The war is the first major conflict among sophisticated cyberspace actors, and some observers predicted that cyberspace operations would feature prominently in combat. This was a reasonable prediction. Russian military doctrine stresses the importance of information dominance, and analysts have spent years sounding the alarm about the potential for large-scale digital disruption in the event of war. Pre-war intrusions against Ukrainian infrastructure seemed like test drives for wartime attacks; not only did Russia express a clear doctrinal interest in offensive cyberspace operations, but it had studied the target for years in advance.

There are more general reasons why we might have expected the war to feature a barrage of cyberspace operations, including sabotage against Ukrainian information systems, institutions and infrastructure.[40] The digital domain is complex and inter-connected, making it possible for attackers to obscure their activities and operate from afar. Attackers also benefit from the growing number of operations at their disposal, includ-ing website defacement, data wiping and sabotage against physical systems.

Defence is difficult for states like Ukraine with extensive information infrastructure. Networks linking government agencies, military organisations and defence firms increase the danger that intrusions can spread laterally. Highly digit-ised states rely on staggering amounts of code, some of which is inevitably flawed and vulnerable. People and organisa-tions would need to remain extraordinarily vigilant to defend themselves in this environment, but people and organisations are fallible. Security lapses make it harder to defend reliably against committed attackers.

Warnings of devastating attacks are commonplace. David Sanger of the *New York Times* calls cyberspace operations 'the perfect weapon' for debilitating infrastructure.[41] Nicole Perlroth, also of the *Times*, warns that such attacks may be cata-clysmic. Her 2021 book, which pays close attention to Russian cyberspace activities, is called *This Is How They Tell Me the World Ends*.[42] Others, however, have challenged these assump-tions. Peacetime harassment is easy, they note, but ambitious operations against hardened military networks are not.

Access to target networks is often tenuous, and malware relies on highly specific intelligence. Attackers risk exposure as their objectives grow, meaning that defenders are more likely to spot their preparations in advance. Effective cyberspace operations in war are not impossible, but they require a rare combination of time, money, skill, organisation and luck.[43]

Wartime operations are also difficult because states pay closer attention to their defences when under attack. Pre-war preparations include hardening existing networks and building redundant communications. They also include moving data onto the cloud and away from domestic servers, which are vulnerable to cyber and physical attack. And they can call on foreign allies and private firms for technical support; the barriers to public–private cooperation are lower when civilians are at risk.

The Russia–Ukraine war (ongoing as of late 2024) presents an early test of opposite claims. If cyberspace operations are potentially decisive in conflict, then we should have seen Russia and Ukraine employing them with great energy in the early days of the war – and succeeding. In this case, then we could say that the hopes and fears of strategists in this new domain were entirely justified. Perhaps there is something fundamentally different about cyberspace that causes states to treat digital innovations differently from other emerging technologies. But if there is evidence that Russia and Ukraine took a more cautious approach, or if their cyberspace efforts proved disappointing, then we may be witnessing the old pattern of hope and fear followed by resignation.

Microsoft was among the first to take stock of cyber operations in the war, issuing two reports on Russian activity in summer 2022.[44] Its data suggests that most Russian activities are about stealing information and influencing the public debate, not incapacitating information systems or causing physical harm. Microsoft's reporting also suggested a correlation between cyberspace operations and conventional campaigns, highlighting a half-dozen instances in which malware moved on a target in advance of military forces. Yet the link was tenuous, and in some cases Russian cyberspace efforts were simply aimed at gathering information. Efforts to use malware to disable Ukraine's military or its foreign partners were infrequent and inconsequential. Most operations were related to espionage and propaganda, with a smattering of sabotage. There is little evidence in open sources that cyberspace operations had a meaningful effect on Ukraine's combat performance in the opening stages of the war, or that they had much effect on the international response.

Many analysts have subsequently assessed the effects of cyberspace operations.[45] Most agree on the basics. Russia has been quite active in cyberspace, using it as a source of intelligence and a vehicle for propaganda, but the battlefield results have been marginal. In some ways new technologies have proven to be important, especially drones. Yet in other respects the war looks like a morbid replay of the First World War, with both sides racing to build trench lines and minefields in the hope of exhausting and outlasting their enemies.[46] Russian forces never achieved the dramatic results that some commentators expected before the war.

Why not? Aid from foreign partners and the private sector may have provided a critical bulwark against digital aggression.[47] Or perhaps Ukraine's defenders were better than expected.[48] Maybe Russia restrained its activities because it feared destroying the networks it would need after occupying the country, or because it didn't think that large-scale attacks would be necessary.[49] Maybe Russia withheld operations against the West because it wanted to use the threat of cyberspace attacks to coerce Ukraine's supporters.[50] Russian cyber activities might have been ineffective because they were too reliant on hackers whose activities the Russian state cannot fully control.[51]

There is surely truth in these claims, but there is also a more basic explanation. Because cyberspace is an information domain, cyberspace operations are about gaining information advantages. Intelligence agencies scour the domain in search of details that may be useful to strategists, diplomats and military leaders. They want to know about the strength and disposition of enemy forces, as well as the capabilities and intentions of third parties. In this sense, Russian cyberspace activities are no different from intelligence gathering in past conflicts. Espionage is essential in war; sabotage is marginal. The more that states come to this conclusion, the more they will become resigned to the limits of cyberspace operations as war-fighting instruments.[52]

## Imagining wartime cyber attacks

How will China use cyberspace in a potential war with the US? Will it view the Russian case as a cautionary tale, scaling back its expectations for digital victory and thinking about war in traditional terms? Or will it conduct aggressive operations in the hope of achieving a rapid low-cost triumph? And who will suffer most? Will a Chinese wartime campaign target US military forces, US allies, US civilian infrastructure or some mix of all three?

US officials are increasingly concerned about Chinese cyberspace preparations.[53] They seem convinced that China has not been discouraged by Russia's poor performance in the Ukraine war. On the contrary, they have issued stark warnings about how China will exploit cyberspace in the case of war. In February 2024, the Office of the Director of National Intelligence highlighted the danger that China could use cyberspace against soldiers and civilians alike. 'If Beijing believed that a major conflict with the United States were imminent', it concluded, 'it would consider aggressive cyber operations against US critical infrastructure and military assets. Such a strike would be designed to deter US military action by impeding US decision-making, inducing societal panic, and interfering with the deployment of US forces.'[54] Operations against civilian infrastructure would represent a major expansion for China in cyberspace, where it is best known for espionage.[55]

Chinese doctrine views cyberspace as critical in war, where information control will loom large in what it calls 'systems confrontation'.[56] Injecting confusion into US military operations will make it harder to organise a response. US leaders might be discouraged from fighting if they worry that their forces will not have a clear view of the battlespace. Attacks on information systems are particularly worrisome, given that China has also developed an impressive suite of 'anti-access' weapons against incoming maritime and air forces. The idea of steaming towards a fight against an adversary with such weapons is unsettling; the thought of doing it without situational awareness is frightening. China may believe that such fears will deter Washington from coming to the defence of Taiwan or other regional partners.[57]

Cyberspace operations surely appeal to Chinese strategists. The US military relies on an interconnected architecture among its various forces in theatre. This enables coordination over vast distances, but it potentially creates multiple points of vulnerability. China may believe it can take advantage of US dependence on information technologies to disable or degrade US communications. But there are limits to what China can expect. Successful cyberspace operations require elaborate efforts to conceal malware before it is unleashed upon target systems, because exposure gives defenders the opportunity to take preventive action. Successful attacks, however, require a large organisational investment in intelligence-gathering, target acquisition, exploit development and execution. The more that China hopes to achieve, the more likely it will be discovered in advance. It may be able to conceal more modest efforts, but those will do less harm to US military forces.

This speaks to a more fundamental problem. In peacetime, attackers have the advantage of choosing among many possible targets and they can take their time. Defenders in peacetime are also less vigilant and they spread resources more broadly. Everything is different in war. In a deep crisis preceding violence, states are likely to put a premium on network defence, especially if they are counting on reliable communications for conventional military campaigns. Cyber-security professionals will be on guard, and they will almost certainly focus on hardening critical networks. Moreover, attackers will lose the luxury of time as military action draws near. Significant effects require methodically developing intrusion plans and malware payloads based on specific intelligence on key networks. In a shooting war there will be a lot less time for such efforts. This suggests that the effects of offensive cyberspace operations will decline quickly.

Although Chinese doctrine continues to emphasise the importance of controlling information in the early stages of conflict, Chinese strategists may be aware of the limits of offensive cyberspace operations in war. Indeed, they may have a back-up plan. Instead of focusing on elegant operations against military communications, China may attempt to coerce the US through attacks on civilian infrastructure.

Such attacks would seek to undermine public morale by degrading physical capabilities. Targeting the utilities that civilians take for granted might cause the public to demand peace, or at least question the value of the object at stake in the war. Defending democratic Taiwan is admirable in theory, but Americans may get cold feet if they worry that society will fall apart. If that sounds melodramatic, consider the 2024 congressional testimony from the CISA's director, Easterly, at a hearing on Chinese cyberspace activities.

Easterly did not mince words. In a hypothetical war, she warned that multiple simultaneous infrastructure attacks could produce 'social panic … at a massive scale'. Operations against utilities and the financial sector are particularly unnerving.

Civilians might respond badly if they suddenly lose access to power, clean water and money.[58]

Other officials are sounding the alarm. The congressionally mandated Cyberspace Solarium Commission Report began with a fictional 'Warning from Tomorrow'. The commissioners asked readers to imagine life in Washington in the aftermath of a catastrophic attack. Not only would residents live in desolation and danger, but they would probably lose faith in the government. Support for a distant war might disappear. The US priority in such an awful scenario would be rescuing citizens, rebuilding infrastructure and restoring social cohesion. Because fighting a war on the other side of the world might seem less important, China's leaders may believe they can use the threat of infrastructure attacks to deter the US from intervening in a crisis. Perhaps they believe that the best way to pressure leaders of a democratic country is by imposing costs on the people living there.

The turn from military networks to civilian infrastructure is akin to the expansion of strategic bombing in the Second World War. Pre-war US doctrine was based on the idea that bombing raids against Germany's vital industrial nodes would cause its economy to falter.[59] Germany's tightly interlocked economy made it appear particularly vulnerable to cascading effects. But practical problems (bad maps, inaccurate bombs, lethal air defences) got in the way of this vision. As the war progressed, the allies increasingly turned to large-scale bombing raids against urban centres. While US strategists never gave up on the hope of using airpower to undermine the German war economy, the limits of technology encouraged a shift towards a different theory of victory. Undermining civilian morale became as important as destroying the industrial foundation of Germany's war machine.

Historians continue to debate the strategic effects of allied bombing. German civilians did not rise up against the Nazi regime even after massive raids on Hamburg and Dresden. The economy also proved surprisingly resilient under pressure and bombers faced serious technical problems that inhibited range and accuracy. Others, however, argue that bombing ultimately did have important effects on German capabilities, especially after the allies were able to target oil and synthetic-fuel facilities. Scholars have also found evidence that German leaders were increasingly concerned about a social breakdown as the bombing intensified.[60]

What does this tell us, if anything, about alleged Chinese preparations for cyberspace operations against American infrastructure? Does it suggest that China is relying on an old theory of victory in a radically new technological domain? And if so, are US officials right to sound the alarm? Are cyber attacks against civilian targets really capable of undermining society? Are they really enough to cause the US to back down in a crisis or conflict?

Chinese strategists may view the US alarm as proof of concept. The fact that preparations have already stoked American fears implies that wartime operations will have powerful coercive effects. They may also be encouraged by the oft-heard warnings among US engineers that the information systems that connect public infrastructure are outmoded and insecure.[61] The combination of physical vulnerability and public alarm suggests that China has a window of opportunity and that it can use cyberspace operations in the US instead of risking everything on a direct confrontation with US military forces.

That said, China's efforts may prove disappointing. One reason is that cyberspace operations may not cause extensive damage. It is true that infrastructure networks offer a large attack surface to would-be attackers, but the effects of operations are often hard to predict in advance. As discussed above, cyberspace operations are not target-agnostic in the manner of conventional munitions. Attackers develop specific tools against specific systems; these are *sui generis* weapons designed to produce certain effects. For this reason, lessons learned from previous operations may not be applicable and operations may fizzle for unknown reasons.[62] Moreover, US infrastructure providers may be able to restore service relatively quickly, especially if they have government assistance. Unlike massive bombing raids, the consequences of cyberspace operations may be temporary and reversible. Policymakers are paying more attention to resilience and public–private coordination. Successful efforts will improve damage mitigation and reduce the consequences of cyber attacks.[63]

Unless China is able to cause extensive and lasting damage to infrastructure, there is little reason to believe that this will serve as a useful coercive tool. Recent research has pointed out the limits of cyberspace coercion; physical attacks tend to be much more compelling.[64] And even if China is able to grab Americans' attention, the reaction could work against Chinese strategy. Rather than clamouring for a settlement, the public might demand revenge.

\*   \*   \*

The US and China have competing visions for the international order. Their visions are fundamentally incompatible. The US has spent 80 years crafting a global system in its image, building institutions, extolling the virtues of trade and encouraging the spread of democracy. Sometimes it has sacrificed these norms in the pursuit of naked self-interest, but even in those cases it justified its illiberal policies as necessary aberrations in the service of the long-term good.[65] American leaders are proud to have helped transform maritime East Asia into a haven for democracies and a regional economic powerhouse. Threats to the status quo are thus ideological as well as material: an illiberal hegemon would threaten to roll back democracy and undermine prosperity. It would also upend the international balance of power, given the increasing importance of Asia to the global economy.

The view from Beijing is different. Chinese leaders find the status quo intolerable. The United States' network of military bases and regional allies does not feel like the foundation of a stable regional order; it feels like a cordon that keeps China from enforcing its maritime claims. US military power also backstops Taiwanese autonomy and prevents China from resolving a core national interest. And, as long as the US is first among equals in international institutions, China will struggle to expand its political influence.

The US is pursuing a grand strategy of the status quo; China is pursuing a grand strategy of revision. Emerging technologies are fundamental to both great powers' theory of security. Washington believes that new technologies facilitate trade and finance, and enable power projection. A durable forward military posture, along with the ability to rapidly move forces from place to place, deters challengers and provides security in key regions.[66] Beijing believes that new technologies offer pathways to economic growth and political clout. It also believes that military innovations make it possible to deter the US from intervening in a regional conflict. The ability to keep US forces at bay might give it leverage over other Asian powers who have long relied on US protection.

Technology also looms large for strategists in the event of war. Strategists pay close attention when new technologies open up the possibility of fighting in new domains. Such moments lead to speculation that key innovations will enable fundamental changes in war fighting that make decisive victory possible. Painful wartime lessons, however, reveal the limits of novel weapons and platforms.

Something similar may be playing out in cyberspace today. Notions of cyber war imply an antiseptic style of fighting, where victory and defeat depend more on savvy information campaigns than on military violence. This is understandably appealing, especially for those who bear the responsibility of ordering soldiers into conflict. Yet the limits of offensive cyberspace operations are becoming clearer and states are spending more on defence. Russia's disappointing performance in Ukraine also suggests that cyberspace operations, while potentially important in the context of a broader campaign, may be limited as stand-alone strategic tools.

Cyberspace will surely play an important role in possible future great-power war, given the ubiquity of digital communications and automated systems among the great powers. But if the track record of other technological breakthroughs is any guide, then offensive cyberspace operations are unlikely to prove decisive. Chinese strategists may not have come to this conclusion, however. It is possible that they attribute Russia's failure to other causes, and still trust that their approach to the domain is correct. If this is the case, then Chinese leaders have not acknowledged the strategic limits of cyberspace operations.

What might cause them to lose faith? China's adversaries may engage in sabotage that calls Beijing's cyber capabilities into question. Sabotage is the weaponisation of organisational friction.[67] It includes a variety of efforts to decrease adversary efficiency, morale and self-confidence. Selective sabotage against Chinese information systems may not have dramatic effects, but it may plant a seed of doubt about the reliability of cyberspace operations. If a peacetime sabotage campaign succeeds, China would be less likely to provoke a crisis. But if it fails, then losing a war might be the surest way to puncture Chinese confidence. The experience of losing exposes pre-war strategic fallacies, as described in Chapter Two, and forces hard conversations about the underlying sources of national power. Wartime failure, however painful, may be necessary to learn the limits of technologies in new war-fighting domains. In this way it can put the state's grand strategy on firmer ground – assuming the government can withstand the political consequences of defeat.

None of this is to suggest that the US has taken a more relaxed view. Civilian and military leaders have repeatedly expressed their belief that mastery of new technologies is essential for victory in future conflicts. This requires improving cyberspace operations in conventional war fighting; integrating AI; exploiting the gains of the precision revolution; and figuring out how to protect satellites against increasingly sophisticated ASAT weapons. They hope that technological progress, long a point of pride in Washington, will allow US forces to establish information dominance in the early days of fighting. It will not have to rely on material advantages or mobilise for grinding, protracted wars. It will not have to shift to a wartime economy or return to a conscript army. Technology will allow the US to fight on its own terms – and win. At the same time, they remain deeply concerned that China is poised to race ahead in key technologies. They issue dire warnings about Chinese cyber-space activities, AI investments and space capabilities. They worry that the American lead is a wasting asset.

Neither China nor the US appears to be resigned to the practical limits of new war-fighting tools, or to the organisational problems that will reduce their combat effectiveness. Hope and fear still rule the day. This does not mean that they have broken the historical pattern described above, wherein moments of innovation produce intense emotional reactions that attenuate over time. What it means is that leaders on both sides are still coming to grips with the uses and limits of their new capabilities. Put another way, they are still in the learning process. The danger is that they will act rashly before the process is complete.

# Open questions

This book describes the relationship between strategy (a theory of victory) and grand strategy (a theory of security), using a series of case studies to illustrate how these concepts interact. Five themes stand out.

Firstly, strategic blunders can undermine an otherwise effective grand strategy. Wartime delusions encourage wasteful and counterproductive strategic choices that leave the state worse off. In the years leading up to the Peloponnesian War, Athens and Sparta had forged grand strategies that played to their strategic advantages and were cognisant of their comparative weaknesses. Athens made itself secure by building a dominant navy and pursuing maritime commerce, all the while protecting the city and its port with strong defensive walls. As it grew, Athens co-opted smaller city-states into the Delian League, which included tributary allies and colonies. Commercial revenue and tribute fed Athens' continued naval expansion, setting in motion a virtuous cycle which could, in theory, have led to a long era of stability and security.

What Athens did not possess was an army capable of taking on Sparta and the rival Peloponnesian League. Spartan dominance was a powerful deterrent to would-be invaders, and it allowed Sparta to concentrate on sustaining the most powerful army in the ancient Greek world. This fit logically with Sparta's grand strategy, which was based on sustaining its slave-based regime. Spartan leaders were cautious about sending its army far from home, fearing that doing so would inspire a slave rebellion. Staying at home made sense, given these priorities, especially because the economy did not depend on foreign commerce.

In the run-up to the Peloponnesian War, however, both Greek great powers convinced themselves that they could fight and win without challenging their enemy's comparative advantage. The first few years of fighting revealed their strategic ideas as delusional, yet neither side was willing to seek a genuine peace. The result was a prolonged and exhausting war that put Athens and Sparta at risk of predation from outside powers. Fundamentally misguided strategies undermined what had been effective grand strategies. Athens' defeat was the beginning of the end of its golden age. Sparta's victory was a temporary triumph with terrible consequences.

Secondly, strategy and grand strategy sometimes work at cross purposes. France implemented an exceptional strategy in the American War of Independence, combining joint and combined operations with adroit diplomacy to overcome British forces. France's support for the upstart Americans was particularly noteworthy, given the vast ideological gulf between the monarchy and the republican insurgency. Yet its strategic victory was counterproductive for grand strategy because the costs of fighting put stress on the treasury that the monarchy ultimately could not bear. Moreover, the positive effects of victory on the international balance of power were fleeting. France did not really secure itself against Great Britain; it just went broke.

Britain's strategic debacle, by contrast, was a blessing for its grand strategy. The country was slowly building the underlying institutional infrastructure of naval imperialism before the American revolution. The war delayed the process, slowing badly needed naval reforms and sowing internal divisions among political and military leaders. But losing – and losing dramatically – forced British leaders to reconsider the foundations of their security. The shocking defeat energised their efforts to modernise the Royal Navy and build an administrative apparatus that could organise a globe-spanning empire.

Thirdly, uncertain grand strategies produce half-hearted wartime strategies. Sometimes states go to war without a clear sense of the value of the political object. That is, they don't quite know how victory will enhance security. Because they are unsure, they are unwilling to make hard choices among strategic alternatives. Instead of articulating a clear and consistent theory of victory, they hedge, which compounds their sense of doubt and encourages more infighting among military leaders. This was the case for Great Britain in the American war, which was characterised from the start by divisions between the king, the cabinet and Parliament. Profound questions about the value of the American colonies undermined Britain's unity of effort and led to deep strategic confusion in the war itself.

The same problem affected the United States' strategy in the Vietnam War. US leaders made key strategic decisions during the period after the Cuban Missile Crisis and before detente. Traditional fears about communist expansion still occupied the White House in these critical years, even though the aftermath of the Cuban episode relaxed tensions among the superpowers. President Lyndon Johnson was particularly torn about Vietnam. Unwilling to abandon South Vietnam but fearful of escalation, he sent a growing force to the conflict but then tried to restrain it. The administration gradually increased the use of airpower, for instance, but it also kept a close eye on the target list out of fear of inadvertently drawing China deeper into the war. Unsurprisingly, this led to frustration among political and military leaders. Desperate for ways to compel Hanoi to settle the conflict without seeing it spin out of control, the administration invested in long-shot covert operations that were tragic failures. Contemporary debates about the causes of strategic failure in Vietnam focus on institutional short-comings (e.g., the military's conventional biases that kept it from adopting effective counter-insurgency methods), but the fundamental problem was a grand strategy in flux.

Fourthly, military decisions are not always sensible in terms of strategy, even if they make sense in terms of grand strategy. The debate over nuclear weapons is a case in point. Scholars have argued for decades about the nuclear-revolution theory, which holds that the costs and risks of nuclear use overwhelm the value of any conceivable political object, making strategy absurd. Furthermore, the extraordinary destructiveness of nuclear weapons should encourage states to change how they think about national security. A modest arsenal should be enough to create a sense of security and reduce the need for arms racing or ambitious military planning. Nuclear-armed states, however, have not behaved this way. In the Cold War, the US and the Soviet Union engaged in an intense and lasting arms race, and they never accepted the idea that mutual nuclear deterrence would keep them safe. Yet they never used nuclear weapons in anger, despite their deep mutual hostility. Such restraint is historically abnormal. States usually try to use new weapons when they can.

Distinguishing strategy and grand strategy helps to resolve the debate over the nuclear revolution. The theory fails the historical test in terms of grand strategy. State behaviour simply did not follow its logical prescriptions in terms of force structure, attitudes towards missile defence, fears of proliferation and so on. But the fact that leaders refused to actually use nuclear weapons is striking, and it suggests that the nuclear revolution has profound implications at the level of strategy.

Distinguishing strategy and grand strategy also sheds light on the debate over counter-terrorism. The US approach after 9/11 has come under withering criticism for its apparent strategic drift. US leaders have struggled to define what 'victory' means against groups like al-Qaeda and the Islamic State. Wars usually end through coercion or conquest, but neither is likely against transnational groups animated by millennial visions and martyrdom. Strategy is logically impossible without a vision of victory. Grand strategy, however, seeks not victory but security. There is no objective goal, only a subjective feeling of safety. This helps explain the open-ended commitment to counter-terrorism, despite the lack of a clear objective. US forces seek to keep the threat of terrorism at a reasonably low level, even if they cannot eliminate the threat completely. This is akin to police work. Police forces do not put an end to crime, but they can reduce its frequency and violence.

In an important sense, the current US approach is similar to British 'air policing' in the interwar period. Both countries sought low-cost methods of subduing non-state threats, at a time in which they faced growing threats from rival great powers. They also sought to exploit new technologies against their less sophisticated targets. For London this meant the novel use of airpower. For the US this means drones, sensors and precision munitions. Ultimately, the British airpower advantage was not enough: a second world war overwhelmed the empire. The US may also eventually face economic limits to its power, forcing it to reconsider the grand-strategic basis of its global war on terrorism.

Fifthly, breakthrough technological innovations lead to similar reactions among strategists and grand strategists. Radical new war-fighting tools inspire hopes of winning quick and decisive victories – but they also lead to fears of sudden and devastating defeat. Experience with the practical problems that accompany new technologies, however, leads to more modest aspirations and less intense concerns. Strategists become resigned to the limits of new technologies, even if they still find them useful. The same pattern of hope, fear and resignation describes the effect of new technologies on grand strategy. Innovations that loom just over the horizon cause observers to speculate that technological mastery will ensure long-term security. At the same time, they worry about falling into a position of long-term danger if their adversaries leap ahead. But, as with strategy, these hopes and fears attenuate over time.

We have seen this pattern in the response to the advent of blue-ocean warships, strategic bombers, and orbiting satellites. More recently, we have seen a glimpse of it in cyberspace, where the hopes and fears surrounding cyber war seemed to give way to a more relaxed attitude. Ongoing tensions between the US and China, however, have renewed the fear of devastating cyberspace operations. Whether this is a brief panic or an enduring strategic concern remains to be seen. So too does the question about perceived offensive advantages. Those who worry about suffering from cyber attacks may also believe that digital offensives can substitute for physical violence, reducing the potential costs of conflict.

Strategists who hold these beliefs are more likely to choose war, with all the risks that entails.

* * *

The analysis of strategy and grand strategy can be applied to other wars, ongoing at the time of writing. In some cases, strategy and grand strategy are aligned, as with Ukraine's defence against Russia. Ukraine's grand strategy over the last decade has focused on an effort to win more Western support, which it hopes will culminate in NATO membership. Its wartime approach is no different, as it relies heavily on Western aid to offset Russian military superiority. Ukraine has aggressively courted support from European members and the US, both to win the war and to secure the country in the aftermath. They have also reached out to the private sector for strategic and grand-strategic reasons. The immediate strategic value of private partnerships is most clear in terms of information security. Deals with private information-technology firms allowed Ukraine to move government data to the cloud in bulk before the Russian invasion, which may have helped it reduce the danger of cyberspace attacks. Durable partnerships with multi-national firms may also help the economy recover when the war ends, and in so doing provide a more durable foundation for national defence. Ukrainian leaders deserve praise for aligning its strategy and grand strategy.

Russian decisions, by contrast, appear to be contradictory. Russian grand strategy before the war seemed designed to slowly erode Western cohesion, in part by rhetorically challenging the US-led 'rules-based order' and playing on general dissatisfaction with the wars in Iraq and Afghanistan. The February 2022 invasion was inconsistent with this grand strategy, not least because it breathed new life into NATO. Why Russian President Vladimir Putin chose this course is unclear. He might have become impatient with his grand-strategic approach, he might have become too optimistic about an easy victory over Ukraine, or both. Whatever the reason, the decision to invade has been enormously costly. Some estimate that Russia has suffered a half-million casualties in the war, including as many as 150,000 dead.[1] It has also faced international condemnation, and its economy appears increasingly dependent on Chinese trade and investment.

Russia's theory of victory shifted from rapid conquest to a grinding war of attrition, though this was clearly not its preference. The question now is whether the Kremlin can bring its strategy back into alignment with a reconfigured theory of security. Perhaps it can. Russia now seems to be betting on the idea that a long war will sap the West's will to continue supporting Ukraine's defence. Kyiv is also stuck in a stalemate, after all, and does not have a clear path to victory. Russian officials may believe that Ukraine's supporters will force it to accept a settlement, especially if their politics veers towards the populist right. If so, then it is possible that Russia can gain a reasonably favourable settlement to the war – though at an exorbitant cost. This strategy, moreover, would be broadly consistent with a grand strategy that focused on supporting friendly political parties abroad. A theory of security based on political influence rather than overt military action would be sensible, especially given the extraordinary military costs Russia has suffered in the last two years.

Finally, the analysis of strategy and grand strategy might reveal something about the origins of the war in Gaza, though it is difficult to make firm conclusions in the first year of an ongoing conflict. Israel's theory of security changed after the failure of Camp David negotiations in 2000 and the al-Aqsa intifada (the Palestinian uprising in 2000–05). Israeli leaders, already weary of Yassir Arafat, became wary of Palestinian negotiators in general. The Israeli position hardened after Hamas seized power in Gaza in 2007 and consolidated its rule. Faced with incorrigible groups dedicated to Israel's demise, Israeli leaders reconsidered their theory of security. The answer was to downplay negotiations and focus on physical defences. No lasting peace could come from negotiations with untrustworthy counterparts. Better to make Israel impregnable, prevent Palestinians from uniting under a single party and 'mow the grass' in occasional operations to reduce enemy capabilities.[2] Perhaps Palestinian officials would moderate over time, though when if ever such a change would occur was a mystery. In the meantime, Israel would harden its defences and contain its foes.

Whatever one thinks of this grand strategy, it was at least coherent. The problem was that it absolved Israel from having to devise a theory of victory in the event of war. When Hamas attacked on 7 October, Israel scrambled to piece together its strategic response. Israeli leaders left no doubt that they would go to war to remove Hamas from power, but they could not say what Gaza would look like in the aftermath. In the absence of a clearly defined political goal, some US officials privately grumbled that Israel has resorted to 'whack-a-mole' bombing against Hamas targets. Remarkably, some senior Israeli officials publicly castigated their own government for its unwillingness to imagine the outlines of an acceptable post-Hamas regime.[3] Israel's grand strategy, however practical in peacetime, was proving to be an obstacle to strategy in war. Having invaded Gaza, it had no ready answers to classic strategic questions:

How far do we go militarily? How much do we demand politically? Who will rule the peace?

*   *   *

There are large literatures on strategy and grand strategy. We know a great deal about theories of victory and theories of security. We know less about how they interact. This book is a first cut at the problem; it is certainly not the last word. Indeed, the themes discussed above pose as many questions as they answer.

One question is about the causes of success. Most of the cases in this book have explored famous failures. For a variety of reasons, the Athenians, Spartans, French, British and Americans all struggled to align strategy and grand strategy. Alliance pressures, domestic politics and leadership psychology all played a role. Were they doomed to failure, given all the factors that complicated their choices? If not, what could they have done differently? Why did states ignore signs that their strategic choices were counterproductive for grand strategy, even if they were appealing in the context of war? These counterfactuals can help get a more granular sense of the causes of breakdown. They might also suggest some lessons for avoiding them.

A related question is about how states make the most of strategic failure. Great Britain's ability to recover after the American debacle is a model of transforming wartime loss into peacetime gain. A deeper historical examination of the British experience and other similar cases might help shed light on the question of resilience – an issue of great interest among policymakers today. In the US, the last two presidential administrations have included resilience as a priority in their national-security strategies. Think tanks and government agencies have spent a great deal of time and effort considering the various ways that institutions can improve their resilience. Additional studies have discussed the nature of social resilience in the wake of natural catastrophes or foreign attacks. What I have in mind here is different: how to bounce back from strategic failure in ways that strengthen long-term grand strategy. This is not easy, given the trauma associated with losing. But careful efforts to reconstruct events can lead to grand strategies built on firmer logical foundations. Scholars might usefully ask about the conditions that make a productive examination possible. Policymakers and civil servants might ask how they can facilitate the process – and insulate it from partisan sniping.

A third question has to do with the issue of grand-strategic uncertainty. As discussed in the chapters on Britain in the American revolution and the US in Vietnam, the unsettled grand strategies produced unsettled wartime strategies. The costs for both countries were clear: neither was able to execute a consistent approach, and both descended into vicious infighting as the wars went on. At the same time, there were some inadvertent benefits in uncertainty, because in both cases it legitimised political opposition and enabled withdrawal from costly conflicts. British parliamentarians like Edmund Burke and Charles James Fox provided powerful rhetorical justification for those who sought to make peace and refocus British grand strategy. American congressmen like William Fulbright similarly found space to criticise the war effort, which he worried would metastasise into a much larger conflict. US obligations to Saigon would have been overwhelmed in such an event, with serious implications for US interests.[4]

Neither the British nor the Americans paid a high long-term cost for their withdrawals, no matter how painful they were in the moment. Both would have surely paid a lot more for staying. The costs of grand-strategic uncertainty are real, to be sure, but it does serve as a check on strategic myopia. Grand-strategic clarity enables consistent strategy, but grand-strategic ambiguity allows for reassessment. Scholars can articulate these trade-offs and theorise the effects in different circumstances. Policymakers can be explicit about their own beliefs, whether they are fixed or flexible. A self-conscious evaluation of grand strategy is helpful in wartime, because signs of strategic distress might reflect a deeper issue.

These are only sample questions that flow from strategy and grand strategy. There are many others. None are easy. We can theorise the causes of strategy–grand strategy breakdowns and the conditions that enable success, but testing those theories is difficult because of the complexity of war and the challenges of interpreting wartime decisions. The issue calls out for multidisciplinary work, especially among international-relations theorists and diplomatic and military historians. It also demands joint work among scholars in security studies, who have done pathbreaking work in grand strategy; and scholars in strategic studies, who have focused more squarely on the conduct of strategy in war.

# NOTES

## Introduction

1   There is a vast literature on
    strategy. Key works include
    Beatrice Heuser, *The Evolution
    of Strategy: Thinking War from
    Antiquity to the Present* (Cambridge:
    Cambridge University Press, 2010);
    Lawrence Freedman, *Strategy: A
    History* (Oxford: Oxford University
    Press, 2014); and Hal Brands (ed.),
    *The New Makers of Modern Strategy:
    From the Ancient World to the Digital
    Age* (Princeton, NJ: Princeton
    University Press, 2023).

2   There is a vast literature on grand
    strategy. Key works include Lukas
    Milevski, *The Evolution of Modern
    Grand Strategic Thought* (Oxford:
    Oxford University Press, 2016);
    Thierry Balzacq, Peter Dombrowski
    and Simon Reich (eds) *Comparative
    Grand Strategy: A Framework and Cases*
    (Oxford: Oxford University Press,
    2019); Rebecca Friedman Lissner,

    'What Is Grand Strategy? Sweeping a
    Conceptual Minefield', *Texas National
    Security Review*, vol. 2, no. 1, 2018,
    pp. 53–73; Nina Silove, 'Beyond the
    Buzzword: The Three Meanings of
    "Grand Strategy"', *Security Studies*,
    vol. 27, no. 1, 2018, pp. 27–57; and
    Barry R. Posen and Andrew L. Ross,
    'Competing Visions for US Grand
    Strategy', *International Security*, vol.
    21, no. 3, 1996, pp. 5–53.

3   Barry R. Posen, *The Sources of
    Military Doctrine: France, Britain,
    and Germany Between the World
    Wars* (Ithaca, NY: Cornell University
    Press, 1984), p. 13. Strategy and
    grand strategy both face significant
    obstacles to this kind of ends–means
    rationality. See Tami Davis Biddle,
    *Strategy and Grand Strategy: What
    Students and Practitioners Need to
    Know* (Carlisle, PA: Strategic Studies
    Institute, 2015).

## Chapter One

1  This problem has bedevilled leaders from antiquity to the present. The Roman emperor Tiberius understood the danger of imperial overreach and sought to consolidate the empire rather than expand it. This made him deeply unpopular. Recent US presidents have similarly tried to resist pressure from hawks at home, and some of them have ultimately abandoned their cautious instincts. See Iskander Rehman, *Iron Imperator: Roman Grand Strategy Under Tiberius* (Stockholm: Bokförlaget Stolpe, 2024); and Elizabeth Saunders, *The Insiders' Game: How Elites Make War and Peace* (Princeton, NJ: Princeton University Press, 2024).

2  Athanasios Platias and Vasillis Trigkas, 'Themistocles: Leadership and Grand Strategy', in Emmanouil M.L. Economou, Nicholas C. Kyriazis and Athanasios Platias (eds), *Democracy and Salamis: 2500 Years After the Battle That Saved Greece and the Western World* (New York: Springer, 2022), pp. 99–129, at pp. 109–12; and John R. Hale, *Lords of the Sea: The Epic Story of the Athenian Navy and the Birth of Democracy* (New York: Viking, 2009), pp. 3–42.

3  Walter Russell Mead, 'Thucydides, Polybius, and the Legacies of the Ancient World', in Hal Brands (ed.), *The New Makers of Modern Strategy: From the Ancient World to the Digital Age* (Princeton, NJ: Princeton University Press, 2023), pp. 42–66, at pp. 51–2.

4  Other triremes were customised for carrying hoplites and horses. See Hale, *Lords of the Sea*, pp. 86, 149.

5  Nicolle Hirschfeld, 'Trireme Warfare in Thucydides', in Robert B. Strassler (ed.), *The Landmark Thucydides* (New York: Free Press, 1996), pp. 608–13.

6  Donald Kagan, *The Peloponnesian War* (New York: Penguin, 2003), pp. 60–2, 452; and Victor Davis Hanson, *A War Like No Other: How the Athenians and Spartans Fought the Peloponnesian War* (New York: Random House, 2005), p. 27.

7  Strassler, *Landmark Thucydides*, p. 17; and Kagan, *Peloponnesian War*, p. 27.

8  Kagan, *Peloponnesian War*, p. 59.

9  Later in the war Sparta loosened up this practice, and in the last years of the war made inroads against the Athenian navy by buying its rowers with promises of better pay. See Hanson, *War Like No Other*, p. 23.

10  Kagan, *Peloponnesian War*, pp. 57–60.

11  This is not to say that Sparta never projected power. It famously allied with Athens to stave off the Persian threat, and then worked to sustain diplomacy in the Greek world to balance against resurgent Persian power. But its fundamental purpose, as Paul Rahe puts it, was 'to keep their Argive enemies out, the helots down, and the Arcadians, above all others, in'. Paul S. Rahe, *The Spartan Regime: Its Character, Origins, and Grand Strategy* (New Haven, CT: Yale University Press, 2016), p. 123.

12  Kagan, *Peloponnesian War*, pp. 57–8.

13  This discussion draws on Joshua Rovner, 'Sea Power Versus Land Power: Cross-domain Deterrence and the Peloponnesian War', in Jon R. Lindsay and Erik Gartzke (eds), *Cross-domain Deterrence: Strategy in an Era of Complexity* (Oxford: Oxford University Press, 2019); and Joshua Rovner, 'A Long War in the East: Doctrine, Diplomacy, and the Prospects for Protracted US–China Conflict', *Diplomacy & Statecraft*, vol. 29, no. 1, 2018, pp. 129–42.

14  Strassler, *Landmark Thucydides*, pp. 17–28.

15  *Ibid.*, p. 67. Compare this to Churchill's description of Admiral Jellicoe in the First World War: 'the only man on either side who

could lose the war in an afternoon'. Winston S. Churchill, *The World Crisis 1916–1918*, Vol. 3 (New York: Rosetta Books, 2013 [1923]), p. 103.

16  Strassler, *Landmark Thucydides*, pp. 45–7.

17  Much the same occurred in the 1990s, when the United States began to treat the containment regime around Iraq as an end in itself. This had the effect of obscuring the success at removing Iraq as a threat to regional security. Joshua Rovner, 'Delusion of Defeat: The United States and Iraq, 1990–1998', *Journal of Strategic Studies*, vol. 37, no. 4, August 2014, pp. 482–507.

18  Strassler, *Landmark Thucydides*, pp. 80–82, at p. 82.

19  B.H. Liddell Hart, *The Strategy of the Indirect Approach* (London: Faber & Faber, 1941).

20  Kagan, *Peloponnesian War*, pp. 90–6 at p. 94.

21  Sparta's strategy had been more successful in the first Peloponnesian War (460–445 BCE), but in the years that followed Athens had grown wealthy, its navy had grown in size and sophistication, and it had extended and fortified its defensive walls.

22  Strassler, *Landmark Thucydides*, pp. 166–7, 196–8; and Kagan, *Peloponnesian War*, pp. 96, 102–4.

23  Kagan, *Peloponnesian War*, pp. 153, 163–5.

24  Thucydides calculates a somewhat smaller Spartan force. Compare Hanson, *War Like No Other*, p. 155, and Strassler, *Landmark Thucydides*, p. 342.

25  Athenian leaders were mindful of the fact that the battle occurred while Athens and Sparta were under a truce. But the so-called Peace of Nicias of 421 was never much more than a useful fiction, and the peace itself started to break down less than a year after it was signed.

26  Kagan, *Peloponnesian War*, p. 166.

27  Strassler, *Landmark Thucydides*, p. 254.

28  Kagan, *Peloponnesian War*, pp. 179–88.

29  Sparta's hegemony in Greece was brief, and it was eventually defeated by Thebes and Macedon.

30  'What is at stake is more than one small country', Bush declared to Congress during the Gulf War. '[I]t is a big idea: a new world order, where diverse nations are drawn together in common cause to achieve the universal aspirations of mankind – peace and security, freedom, and the rule of law. Such is a world worthy of our struggle and worthy of our children's future.' George H.W. Bush, 'Address Before a Joint Session of the Congress on the State of the Union', 29 January 1991, https://bush41library.tamu.edu/archives/public-papers/2656.

31  Randall Schweller, 'Why Trump Now: A Third Image Explanation', in Robert Jervis et al. (eds), *Chaos in the Liberal Order: The Trump Presidency and International Politics in the Twenty-first Century* (New York: Columbia University Press, 2018), pp. 22–39.

32  Rush Doshi, who until March 2024 served as Deputy Senior Director for China and Taiwan Affairs at the National Security Council, describes China's grand strategy in evolutionary terms. In the 1990s it sought to blunt American power; in the 2000s it sought to build its own; now it seeks to displace the United States. Rush Doshi, *The Long Game: China's Grand Strategy to Displace American Order* (Oxford: Oxford University Press, 2021).

33  Avery Goldstein, 'China's Grand Strategy Under Xi Jinping: Reassurance, Reform, and Resistance', *International Security*, vol. 45, no. 1, Summer 2020, pp. 164–201. For a useful historical overview of China's grand strategy, see Andrew Scobell et al., *China's Grand Strategy: Trends, Trajectories, and Long-term Competition* (Santa Monica, CA:

RAND Corporation, 2020), especially pp. 17–21.

34 Jessica Chen Weiss, 'The China Trap: U.S. Foreign Policy and the Perilous Logic of Zero-sum Competition', *Foreign Affairs*, vol. 101, no. 5, September/October 2022, pp. 40–58.

35 Hal Brands and Michael Beckley, *Danger Zone: The Coming Conflict with China* (New York: W. W. Norton, 2022).

36 David Sacks, 'Why China Would Struggle to Invade Taiwan', Council on Foreign Relations, 10 January 2024, https://www.cfr.org/article/why-china-would-struggle-invade-taiwan.

37 On contested zones, see Barry R. Posen, 'Command of the Commons: The Military Foundation of US Hegemony', *International Security*, vol. 8, no. 1, Summer 2003, pp. 5–46. On the precision revolution, see Thomas G. Mahnken, 'Weapons: The Growth & Spread of the Precision-strike Regime', Daedalus, vol. 140, no. 3, Summer 2011, pp. 45–57.

38 Joshua Rovner, 'Two Kinds of Catastrophe: Nuclear Escalation and Protracted War in Asia', *Journal of Strategic Studies*, vol. 40, no. 5, 2017, pp. 696–730.

39 Francis J. Gavin, *The Taming of Scarcity and the Problems of Plenty: Rethinking International Relations and American Grand Strategy in a New Era* (Abingdon: Routledge for the IISS, 2024).

40 Examples include Andrew F. Krepinevich, Jr, 'Protracted War: A Preliminary Assessment', Center for a New American Security, 5 February 2020, https://www.cnas.org/publications/reports/protracted-great-power-war; and Iskander Rehman, *Planning for Protraction: A Historically Informed Approach to Great-power War and Sino-US Competition* (Abingdon: Routledge for the IISS, 2023).

41 Indeed, he ultimately fell victim to the same tendencies. See Richard K. Betts, 'Not with My Thucydides, You Don't', *American Interest*, 1 March 2007, https://www.the-american-interest.com/2007/03/01/not-with-my-thucydides-you-dont/.

## Chapter Two

1 The commander of the French expeditionary force received a congratulatory letter from Louis XVI after Yorktown. According to his memoir, the king 'directed me to have a public thanksgiving sung at the head of the army, and to order rejoicings on the occasion, as had been done at Paris and throughout France'. Jean-Baptiste Donatien de Vimeur, *Memoirs of the Marshall Count de Rochambeau*, trans. W.E. Wright (Paris: Belin & Co., 1838), p. 80.

2 Robert Middlekauff, *The Glorious Cause: The American Revolution, 1763–1789* (Oxford: Oxford University Press, 2005), p. 402.

3 Samuel Flagg Bemis, *The Diplomacy of the American Revolution* (New York: American Historical Association, 1935), p. 16.

4 Nicholas Tracy, *Navies, Deterrence, and American Independence: Britain and Seapower in the 1760s and 1770s* (Vancouver, BC: University of British Columbia Press, 1988), p. 16; and Jonathan R. Dull, *The French Navy and American Independence: A Study of Arms and Diplomacy, 1774–1787* (Princeton, NJ: Princeton University Press, 1976), pp. 336–7.

5 N.A.M. Rodger, *The Command of the Ocean: A Naval History of Britain, 1649–1815* (New York: W. W. Norton & Co., 2014), pp. 378–9.

6 Middlekauff, *Glorious Cause*, p. 402; and Tracy, *Navies, Deterrence, and American Independence*, p. 16.

7   Tracy, *Navies, Deterrence, and American Independence,* p. 118.

8   Dull, *French Navy*, pp. 44–7.

9   *Ibid.*, p. 21.

10  Spain was important as a naval ally, as we will see below, but it was at best a modest land power.

11  Dull, *French Navy*, pp. 9–10.

12  Tracy, *Navies, Deterrence, and American Independence*, p. 3.

13  Charles Lee Lewis, *Admiral de Grasse & American Independence* (Annapolis, MD: Naval Institute Press, 1945), p. 55; and Tracy, *Navies, Deterrence, and American Independence*, p. 118.

14  Orville T. Murphy, 'Charles Gravier de Vergennes: Profile of an Old Regime Diplomat', *Political Science Quarterly*, vol. 83, no. 3, September 1968, pp. 400–18; and Dull, *French Navy*, pp. 7–8.

15  Sam Willis, *The Struggle for Sea Power: A Naval History of the American Revolution* (New York: W. W. Norton & Co., 2015), p. 4.

16  Tracy, *Navies, Deterrence, and American Independence*, pp. 3, 16, 20–1.

17  Matt J. Schumann, 'Generational Competition in a Multipolar World: William III and André-Hurcule de Fleury', in Hal Brands (ed.), *The New Makers of Modern Strategy: From the Ancient World to the Digital Age* (Princeton, NJ: Princeton University Press, 2023), pp. 295–318, at pp. 310–17.

18  Quoted in Michael Howard, *War in European History* (Oxford: Oxford University Press, 1976), p. 74.

19  Middlekauff, *Glorious Cause*, p. 405; and Dull, *French Navy*, p. 48.

20  Tracy, *Navies, Deterrence, and American Independence*, pp. 121–2.

21  Dull, *French Navy*, pp. 21, 26, 68.

22  John Reeve, 'British Naval Strategy: War on a Global Scale', in Donald Stoker, Kenneth J. Hagan and Michael T. McMaster (eds), *Strategy in the American War of Independence: A Global Approach* (New York: Routledge, 2010), p. 84.

23  Willis, *Struggle for Sea Power*, pp. 214–15; Dull, *French Navy*, p. 19; and Rodger, *Command of the Ocean*, pp. 22–3.

24  Dull, *French Navy*, pp. 151, 316; and Reeve, 'British Naval Strategy', p. 86.

25  Willis, *Struggle for Sea Power*, pp. 218–19.

26  In this sense they anticipated Julian Corbett's ideas about maritime operations: see Julian Corbett, *Some Principles of Maritime Strategy* (Annapolis, MD: Naval Institute Press, 1988 [1911]). For an excellent recent discussion, see Kevin D. McCranie, *Mahan, Corbett, and the Foundations of Naval Strategic Thought* (Annapolis, MD: Naval Institute Press, 2021), pp. 190–201.

27  Lewis, *Admiral de Grasse*, pp. 77–8, 89–90, 110–11. On the British carronade, see Reeve, 'British Naval Strategy', p. 78.

28  Mutual fascination and mutual wariness coloured Franco-American relations before the war. French views of the Americans were not homogeneous, and for some the ideals of the American revolution were intoxicating. But expeditionary troops encountered serious anti-French prejudices on their arrival. See Durand Echevarria, *Mirage in the West: A History of the French Image of American Society to 1815* (Princeton, NJ: Princeton University Press, 1957), pp. 83–6.

29  Middlekauff, *Glorious Cause*, pp. 407–8.

30  Willis, *Struggle for Sea Power*, p. 244.

31  *Ibid.*, pp. 240–51.

32  *Ibid.*, p. 379. Jonathan Abel argues that French thinkers had an important practical impact on the organisation and conduct of the American army. The story that Washington carried a copy of Guibert's *General Essay on Tactics* is probably apocryphal, but it nonetheless reflects French influence during the war. See Jonathan Abel, 'Introduction', in Guibert's *General*

*Essay on Tactics*, trans. Jonathan Abel (London: Brill, 2021), p. xxvii.

33 Middlekauff, *Glorious Cause*, pp. 407–10, 582.

34 The discussion of Yorktown draws on John Ferling, *Almost a Miracle: The American Victory in the War of Independence* (Oxford: Oxford University Press, 2007), pp. 523–39.

35 Stephen Conway, *The War of American Independence, 1775–1783* (London: Edward Arnold, 1995), pp. 69, 157–8.

36 Dull, *French Navy*, pp. 104–5.

37 *Ibid.*, pp. 154–8, 163–4; and James Pritchard, 'French Strategy and the American Revolution: A Reappraisal', *Naval War College Review*, vol. 47, no. 4, Autumn 1994, pp. 83–108, at p. 94.

38 Thomas E. Chávez, *Spain and the Independence of the United States: An Intrinsic Gift* (Santa Fe, NM: University of New Mexico Press, 2002), pp. 198–203.

39 Dull, *French Navy*, p. 340.

40 *Ibid.*, pp. 22–4.

41 Middlekauff, *Glorious Cause*, p. 405. For details, see Jonathan R. Dull, *A Diplomatic History of the American Revolution* (New Haven, CT: Yale University Press, 1985), pp. 52–65.

42 Great powers often tacitly allow their rivals to act covertly in order to reduce the risk of escalation. Austin Carson, *Secret Wars: Covert Conflict in International Politics* (Princeton, NJ: Princeton University Press, 2018).

43 Dull, *French Navy*, pp. 75–94.

44 Tracy, *Navies, Deterrence, and American Independence*, p. 151. Alternatively, France might have been impressed by American prowess. Being convinced that the Americans were good enough to win might have encouraged them to finally make an alliance. See Conway, *War of American Independence*, p. 99.

45 Dull argues that Saratoga was not the cause of French intervention. Instead, he convincingly shows that Vergennes was already sceptical of

the previously limited strategy. The battle, in this sense, was a useful pretext. Dull, *French Navy*, pp. 89–94.

46 *Ibid.*, pp. 97–9.

47 *Ibid.*, p. 110.

48 Lewis, *Admiral de Grasse*, pp. 70–3; and Dull, *French Navy*, p. 124.

49 Dull, *French Navy*, p. 133.

50 Rodger, *Command of the Ocean*, p. 352.

51 Pritchard, 'French Strategy', p. 100.

52 Reeve, 'British Naval Strategy,' p. 92.

53 Dull, *French Navy*, p. 341.

54 On the various European objectives regarding the League, see Leos Müller, 'The League of Armed Neutrality, 1780–1783', in Donald Stoker, Kenneth J. Hagan and Michael T. McMaster (eds), *Strategy in the American War of Independence: A Global Approach* (New York: Routledge, 2009), pp. 202–20. On Vergennes's efforts to bolster the League, see Orville T. Wright, *Charles Gravier: Comte de Vergennes: French Diplomacy in the Age of Revolution, 1719–1787* (Albany, NY: State University of New York Press, 1983), pp. 281–3.

55 One exception was Russia's move to annex Crimea in 1783. According to Matthew Lockwood, the American war distracted France and Great Britain enough to allow Russia to act. This did not, however, affect France's core interest in the continental balance. See Matthew Lockwood, *To Begin the World Over Again: How the American Revolution Devastated the Globe* (New Haven, CT: Yale University Press, 2019), pp. 181–2.

56 Pritchard, 'French Strategy', p. 104.

57 Dull, *French Navy*, pp. 349–50, quoted at p. 350.

58 Conway, *War of American Independence*, pp. 241–2. Because France relied almost entirely on loans to finance the war, it was forced to accept very high interest rates and compressed repayment schedules. See Lockwood, *To Begin the World Over Again*, p. 222.

59 Pritchard, 'French Strategy', p. 87.

60 The following discussion draws on Joshua Rovner, 'History Is Written by the Losers: Strategy and Grand Strategy in the Aftermath of War', *Journal of Strategic Studies* (forthcoming).

61 Nick Bunker, *An Empire on the Edge: How Britain Came to Fight America* (New York: Vintage, 2015), p. 15. For discussions of eighteenth-century British grand strategy, see Paul Kennedy, *The Rise and Fall of British Mastery* (London: Scribner, 1976); and Rodger, *Command of the Ocean*.

62 J.A. Houlding, *Fit for Service: The Training of the British Army, 1715–1795* (Oxford: Clarendon Press, 1981), pp. 19, 395.

63 Rodger, *Command of the Ocean*, p. 368.

64 *Ibid.*, p. 370.

65 *Ibid.*, pp. 370–1.

66 *Ibid.*, p. 369. See also Clive Wilkinson, *The British Navy and the State in the 18th Century* (Suffolk: Boydell Press, 2004), pp. 147–9, and appendix 4.

67 Roger Knight, 'From Impressment to Task Work: Strikes and Disruption in the Royal Dockyards, 1688–1788', in Kenneth Lunn and Ann Day (eds), *History of Work and Labor Relations in the Royal Dockyards* (London: Mansell, 1999), pp. 1–20, at p. 9.

68 Bunker, *Empire on the Edge*, provides an excellent discussion of the crash. For details on the rise of the relationship between war, taxes and the rise of the British administrative state during this time, see John Brewer, *The Sinews of Power: War, Money, and the English State, 1688–1783* (Boston, MA: Unwin Hyman, 1989).

69 Robert Allison, *The American Revolution: A Concise History* (Oxford: Oxford University Press, 2011), p. 5; Samuel Eliot Morrison, *Sources and Documents Illustrating the American Revolution*, 2nd ed. (Oxford: Oxford University Press, 1961), pp. xvii–xxviii; and Houlding, *Fit for Service*, p. 395.

70 Allison, *American Revolution*, p. 1.

71 Andrew Jackson O'Shaughnessy, *The Men Who Lost America: British Leadership, the American Revolution, and the Fate of the Empire* (New Haven, CT: Yale University Press, 2013), pp. 17–46. On the contemporaneous challenge to hereditary monarchs elsewhere in Europe, see David Kaiser, *Politics and War: European Conflict from Philip II to Hitler* (Cambridge, MA: Harvard University Press, 1990), pp. 203–12.

72 Edmund Burke, 'Speech on Conciliation with the Colonies', 22 March 1775, http://press-pubs. uchicago.edu/founders/documents/ v1ch1s2.html; and Charles James Fox, 'Address on the King's Speech: Wars with America and France', 26 November 1778, in F. Warre Cornish (ed.), *The Public School Speaker* (London: John Murray, 1900), pp. 415–16, http://bit.ly/2ylFvHz.

73 Fox, 'Address on the King's Speech'.

74 O'Shaughnessy, *Men Who Lost America*, pp. 97–100; and Middlekauff, *Glorious Cause*, pp. 413–14, 438.

75 O'Shaughnessy, *Men Who Lost America*, pp. 24–5, 67. See also Piers Mackesy, *The War for America, 1775–1783* (Cambridge, MA: Harvard University Press, 1964).

76 Sandwich had been an advocate of strong measures towards the Americans before the war. Like other British hawks, he overestimated the ease of coercing them. O'Shaughnessy, *Men Who Lost America*, p. 326.

77 Conway, *War of American Independence*, pp. 157–8; Mackesy, *War for America*, pp. 524–5; and Dull, *French Navy*, pp. 359–76.

78 Michael Howard, *War in European History* (Oxford: Oxford University Press, 1970), pp. 89–90. It also helped the army, which, despite efforts to increase its size in the mid-eighteenth century, was overstretched and

incapable of sustaining an effective training regime. Committing to a large and distant garrison in North America would have inevitably strained its resources, which were badly needed elsewhere. A more focused army was in a better position to deal with France during the Napoleonic Wars. Houlding, *Fit for Service*, passim.

79 Patrick Karl O'Brien, 'The Formation of a Mercantilist State and the Economic Growth of the United Kingdom, 1453–1815', United Nations University World Institute for Development Economics Research, Research Paper No. 2006/75, July 2006, https://www.wider.unu.edu/sites/default/files/rp2006-75.pdf.

80 Rodger, *Command of the Ocean*, p. 580.

81 Other growing great powers have exhibited the same peculiar combination of ambition and anxiety. See Rovner, 'History Is Written by the Losers'.

## Chapter Three

1 The classic account is Andrew F. Krepinevich, *The Army and Vietnam* (Baltimore, MD: Johns Hopkins University Press, 1988). For a later argument along similar lines, see John A. Nagl, *Learning to Eat Soup with a Knife: Counterinsurgency Lessons from Malaya and Vietnam* (Chicago, IL: University of Chicago Press, 2005).

2 US Army/Marine Corps, *Field Manual 3-24: Counterinsurgency* (Chicago, IL: University of Chicago Press, 2007).

3 Quoted in Fredrik Logevall, *Choosing War: The Lost Chance for Peace and the Escalation of War in Vietnam* (Berkeley, CA: University of California Press, 1999), p. 145. See also Doris Kearns Goodwin, *Lyndon Johnson and the American Dream* (New York: St. Martin's Griffin, 1976), pp. 251–60.

4 Two assessments were particularly noteworthy: 'Memorandum from the Board of National Estimates to the Director of Central Intelligence (McCone)', 9 June 1964, in US State Department Office of the Historian, *Foreign Relations of the United States, 1964–1968, Vietnam 1964*, vol. 1 (Washington DC: United States Government Printing Office, 1992), pp. 484–7; and Board of National Estimates, 'Trends in the World Situation', 8 June 1964, Lyndon Baines Johnson Presidential Library, LBJ Papers, National Security File, Agency File 11–2, CIA.

5 Three years later the CIA director sent the president a memo making the case that the consequences of losing in Vietnam would be manageable. The fact that he insisted on absolute confidentiality speaks to the continuing controversy and disagreement about the goals of the war and its larger relationship to national security. Helms to Johnson, 'Implications of an Unfavorable Outcome in Vietnam', 11 September 1967, reprinted in John K. Allen, John Carver and Tom Elmore (eds), *Estimative Products on Vietnam, 1948–1975* (Washington DC: United States Government Printing Office, 2005), pp. 393–426.

6 John Lewis Gaddis, *Strategies of Containment: A Critical Appraisal of Postwar American National Security Policy* (Oxford: Oxford University Press, 1982), pp. 25–52.

7 On varieties of the domino theory in the Cold War, see Robert Jervis and Jack Snyder (eds), *Dominoes and Bandwagons: Strategic Beliefs and Great Power Competition in the Eurasian Rimland* (New York: Oxford University Press, 1990).

8 President John F. Kennedy was also intrigued by the possibility of special forces while he contemplated US

action in Vietnam. See Geuenter Lewy, *America in Vietnam* (Oxford: Oxford University Press, 1978), p. 20; and David Kaiser, *American Tragedy: Kennedy, Johnson, and the Origins of the Vietnam War* (Cambridge, MA: Harvard University Press, 2000), pp. 68–9.

9  National Security Action Memorandum No. 288, 'Implementation of South Vietnam Programs', 17 March 1964, in US State Department Office of the Historian, *Foreign Relations of the United States, Vietnam 1964*, vol. 1 (Washington DC: United States Government Printing Office, 1992), https://history.state.gov/historicaldocuments/frus 1964-68v01/d87.

10  Robert Pape argues that there was a clear coercive logic to the campaign. US bombers would target North Vietnam's industrial base, thus giving it a reason to come to the table, but they would also 'keep the hostage healthy' in order to emphasise the latent threat of more violence as punishment for non-compliance. And as the campaign became progressively more intense, the US would step up secret diplomacy in order to provide Hanoi an off-ramp when it decided it had had enough. While elements of this programme were clearly present, Pape overstates the degree to which it made up a coherent whole. Indeed, policymakers were continuously at odds with each other (and sometimes with themselves) about the logic of the campaign. See Pape, *Bombing to Win: Air Power and Coercion in War* (Ithaca, NY: Cornell University Press, 1996), pp. 178–81.

11  Austin Carson, *Secret Wars: Covert Conflict in International Politics* (Princeton, NJ: Princeton University Press, 2018), pp. 213–17.

12  This was not controversial among other services. Admiral Ulysses S. Sharp, Commander-in-Chief of US Pacific Command, was a vocal advocate of strategic bombing. Phill Haun, *Tactical Air Power and the Vietnam War: Explaining Effectiveness in Modern Air Warfare* (Cambridge: Cambridge University Press, 2024), pp. 58, 78.

13  Marshall L. Michel III, *The 11 Days of Christmas: America's Last Vietnam Battle* (New York: Encounter Books, 2001), p. 3.

14  The air force later argued that the *Linebacker* bombing campaigns in 1972 validated its beliefs. In reality, airpower's greatest contribution was in its role targeting enemy formations and enabling US and South Vietnam ground offensives. As Phil Haun and Colin Jackson note, 'the USAF had little institutional interest in telling the story of how independent air operations in North Vietnam failed in *Linebacker* I or how *Linebacker* II succeeded only in bringing the North Vietnamese back to Paris to sign an agreement to which they had previously agreed. It had even less incentive to acknowledge the decisive impact of (close air support) and (battlefield air interdiction) missions in the south, as they represented a subordination of air assets to ground commanders.' Haun and Jackson, 'Breaker of Armies: Airpower in the Easter Offensive and the Myth of *Linebacker* I and II in the Vietnam War', *International Security*, vol. 40, no. 3, Winter 2015–16, pp. 139–78, at p. 140.

15  A series of assassinations and government upheavals led Johnson to vent about 'this coup shit'. David M. Barrett, *Uncertain Warriors: Lyndon Johnson and His Vietnam Advisors* (Lawrence, KS: University Press of Kansas, 1993), p. 17.

16  *Operation Market Time* (1965), a Navy and Coast Guard campaign against maritime supply routes, caused the North to increasingly rely on overland lines of communication. These proved much more difficult to interdict. Haun, *Tactical Air Power*, p. 28.

17  Barrett, *Uncertain Warriors*, pp. 17–23.

18  William P. Bundy and John T. McNaughton, 'Courses of Action in Southeast Asia', 21 November 1964, reprinted in US Department of State Office of the Historian, *Foreign Relations of the United States, 1964–1968*, vol. 1, Vietnam 1964, https://history.state.gov/historicaldocuments/frus1964-68v01/d418.

19  Mark Clodfelter, *The Limits of Air Power: The American Bombing of North Vietnam* (Lincoln, NE: University of Nebraska Press, 2006 [1989]), pp. 53–62, 70.

20  Quoted in Clodfelter, *Limits of Air Power*, p. 124.

21  Airpower historians have noted the effectiveness of the bombing in the first campaign, *Linebacker* I, though more recent accounts have challenged the overall impact. Compare Clodfelter, *Limits of Air Power*, pp. 134–46 with Haun, *Tactical Air Power and the Vietnam War*, pp. 192–3.

22  Clodfelter, *Limits of Air Power*, pp. 166–76.

23  Earl H. Tilford, *Crosswinds: The Air Force's Setup in Vietnam* (College Station, TX: Texas A&M Press, 1993), p. xvi. Haun and Jackson make a compelling argument that airpower worked best in support of ground operations. Accepting this idea, however, was difficult for air-force leadership. See Haun and Jackson, 'Breaker of Armies'.

24  On the aftermath of Tet, see Eric Bergerud, *The Dynamics of Defeat: The Vietnam War in Hau Nghia Province* (Boulder, CO: Westview Press, 1991), pp. 215–22. On the aftermath of the Easter Offensive, see Dale Andrade, *America's Last Vietnam Battle: Halting Hanoi's 1972 Easter Offensive* (Lawrence, KS: University Press of Kansas, 2000 [1995]), pp. 284–94. Bergerud and Andrade note that American forces inflicted enormous damage on communist insurgents and the North Vietnamese military, even though they did not resolve the underlying political conflicts fuelling the war.

25  Kennan became a sharp critic of the Johnson administration during the Vietnam War, in part because escalation might inadvertently draw the Soviet Union closer to China at a time when the two were drifting apart. Randall Doyle, 'The Reluctant Heretic: George F. Kennan and the Vietnam War, 1950–1968', *Grand Valley Review*, vol. 27, no. 1, 2004, pp. 54–83, at pp. 73–4.

26  Michel, *11 Days of Christmas*, pp. 164–5; and Tilford, *Crosswinds*, p. 168.

27  Krepinevich, *Army in Vietnam*.

28  Lewis Sorley, *A Better War: The Unexamined Victories and Final Tragedy of America's Last Years in Vietnam* (New York: Harcourt Brace, 1999).

29  Harry G. Summers, *On Strategy: The Vietnam War in Context* (Carlisle Barracks, PA: Strategic Studies Institute, 1982).

30  Letter from Clark M. Clifford to President Johnson, 17 May 1965, reprinted in US Department of State Office of the Historian, *Foreign Relations of the United States, 1964–1968*, vol. 2, Vietnam, January–June 1965 (Washington DC: Government Printing Office, 1996), https://history.state.gov/historicaldocuments/frus1964-68v02/d307#:~:text=I%20believe%20our%20ground%20forces,11%20(Documents%201%E2%80%9310.

31  Barrett, *Uncertain Warriors*, p. 28.

32  Joshua Rovner, *Fixing the Facts: National Security and the Politics of Intelligence* (Ithaca, NY: Cornell University Press, 2011), pp. 66–7.

33  Lt. Gen. Julian J. Ewell and Maj. Gen. Ira A. Hunt, Jr, *Sharpening the Combat Edge: The Use of Analysis to Reinforce Military Judgment* (Washington DC: Department of the Army, 1974).

34  Robert D. Schulzinger, *A Time for War: The United States and Vietnam: 1941–1975* (New York: Oxford University Press, 1996), pp. 182–3.

35 Gregory A. Daddis, *No Sure Victory: Measuring U.S. Army Effectiveness and Progress in the Vietnam War* (Oxford: Oxford University Press, 2015).

36 Frank Leith Jones, *Blowtorch: Robert Komer, Vietnam, and American Cold War Strategy* (Annapolis, MD: Naval Institute Press, 2013), p. 125.

37 Robert Komer, *Bureaucracy Does Its Thing: Institutional Constraints on US–GVN Performance in Vietnam* (Santa Monica, CA: RAND Corporation, 1972).

38 Jones, *Blowtorch*, p. 117.

39 Ibid., p. 139.

40 Ibid., pp. 131–3, 139; and Neil Sheehan, *A Bright Shining Lie: John Paul Vann and America in Vietnam* (New York: Vantage, 1988), pp. 653–4. Sorley argues that the army embraced counter-insurgency and pacification under Westmoreland, and that it was on the path to success. These changes, however, occurred long after the public and Congress had soured on the war. Nor was there much evidence that Saigon had gained the ability to defend itself without an open-ended US security commitment. Sorley, *A Better War*.

41 Stathis N. Kalyvas and Mathew Adam Kocher, 'The Dynamics of Violence in Vietnam, An Analysis of the Hamlet Evaluation System', *Journal of Peace Research*, vol. 46, no. 3, 2009, pp. 335–55.

42 Kenneth Conboy and Dale Andrade, *Spies and Commandos: How America Lost the Secret War in North Vietnam* (Lawrence, KS: University Press of Kansas, 2000); Thomas Ahern, *The Way We Do Things: Black Entry Operations into North Vietnam, 1961–1964* (Washington DC: Center for the Study of Intelligence, 2005); and Robert M. Gillespie, *Black Ops Vietnam: The Operational History of MACVSOG* (Annapolis, MD: Naval Institute Press, 2011).

43 William Rosenau and Austin Long, 'The Phoenix Program and Contemporary Counterinsurgency', 2009, RAND Occasional Paper.

44 Richard Schultz, Jr, *The Secret War Against Hanoi: Kennedy's and Johnson's Use of Spies, Saboteurs, and Covert Warriors in North Vietnam* (New York: HarperCollins, 1999).

45 Carson, *Secret Wars*, p. 201. See also Clayton D. Laurie and Andres Vaart, 'The Republic of Vietnam, Insurgency and Nation-Building, 1954–65', in Laurie and Vaart (eds), *CIA and the Wars in Southeast Asia, 1947–1975* (Washington DC: Center for the Study of Intelligence, 2016), pp. 8–9.

46 Bernard Brodie, *The Absolute Weapon: Atomic Power and World Order* (New York: Harcourt, Brace and Company, 1946), p. 76.

47 Key works articulating the nuclear revolution include Robert Jervis, *The Illogic of American Nuclear Strategy* (Ithaca, NY: Cornell University Press, 1985); Robert Jervis, *The Meaning of the Nuclear Revolution: Statecraft and the Prospect of Armageddon* (Ithaca, NY: Cornell University Press, 1989); Kenneth N. Waltz, *The Spread of Nuclear Weapons: More May Be Better*, Adelphi Paper No. 171 (London: International Institute for Strategic Studies, 1981); and Charles L. Glaser, *Analyzing Strategic Nuclear Policy* (Princeton, NJ: Princeton University Press, 1990).

48 Colin S. Gray and Keith Payne, 'Victory Is Possible', *Foreign Policy*, no. 39, 1980, pp. 14–27. For a famous early critique of the nuclear revolution, see Albert Wohlstetter, 'The Delicate Balance of Terror', *Foreign Affairs*, vol. 37, no. 2, January 1959.

49 See especially Brendan Rittenhouse Green, *The Revolution that Failed: Nuclear Competition, Arms Control, and the Cold War* (Cambridge: Cambridge University Press, 2020); and Keir A. Lieber and Daryl G. Press, *The Myth of the Nuclear Revolution: Power Politics in the Atomic Age* (Ithaca, NY: Cornell University Press, 2020). For a review

of recent critiques, see Paul C. Avey, 'Just Like Yesterday? New Critiques of the Nuclear Revolution', *Texas National Security Review*, vol. 6, no. 2, 2023, pp. 9–31.

50  Francis J. Gavin, 'Strategies of Inhibition: U.S. Grand Strategy, the Nuclear Revolution, and Nonproliferation', *International Security*, vol. 40, no. 1, 2015, pp. 9–46.

51  S. David Broscious, 'Longing for International Control, Banking on American Superiority: Harry S. Truman's Approach to Nuclear Weapons', in John Lewis Gaddis et al. (eds), *Cold War Statesmen Confront the Bomb: Nuclear Diplomacy Since 1945* (Oxford: Oxford University Press, 1999), pp. 18–19.

52  'Memorandum of Discussion at the 257th Meeting of the National Security Council, Washington, August 4, 1955', in *Foreign Relations of the United States, National Security Policy 1955–1957*, vol. 19, https://history.state.gov/historicaldocuments/frus1955-57v19/d30.

53  Philip Nash, 'Bear *Any* Burden? John F. Kennedy and Nuclear Weapons', in Gaddis et al. (eds), *Cold War Statesmen Confront the Bomb*, pp. 120–40, at p. 125.

54  Peter Hayes and Nina Tannenwald, 'Nixing Nukes in Vietnam', *Bulletin of the Atomic Scientists*, May/June 2003, pp. 52–9.

55  Scott D. Sagan and Jeremi Suri, 'The Madman Nuclear Alert: Secrecy, Signaling, and Safety in October 1969', *International Security*, vol. 27, no. 4, Spring 2003, pp. 150–83.

56  Richard Rhodes, *The Making of the Atomic Bomb* (New York: Simon & Schuster, 1986), p. 690.

57  David Holloway, *Stalin and the Bomb: The Soviet Union and Atomic Energy, 1939–1956* (New Haven, CT: Yale University Press, 1994).

58  Sergey Radchenko, 'Moscow's Nuclear Strategy: The Cold War to the Post-Cold War', unpublished

paper prepared for a conference at Curtin University, 'Re-Imagining the Global Nuclear Order', Perth, Australia, January 2024. For a longer discussion of Stalin's foreign policy in the shadow of the bomb, see Sergey Radchenko, *To Run the World: The Kremlin's Cold War Bid for Global Power* (Cambridge: Cambridge University Press, 2024), pp. 46–9, 74–8, 101–5.

59  Vladislav M. Zubok and Hope M. Harrison, 'The Nuclear Education of Nikita Khrushchev', in Gaddis et al. (eds), *Cold War Statesmen Confront the Bomb*, p. 144.

60  Zubok and Harrison, 'The Nuclear Education of Nikita Khrushchev', p. 145.

61  Radchenko, *To Run the World*, p. 316.

62  Nicholas Thompson, 'Nuclear War and Nuclear Fear in the 1970s and 1980s', *Journal of Contemporary History*, vol. 46, no. 1, 2011, pp. 136–49, at p. 138.

63  Keir A. Lieber and Daryl G. Press, 'The New Era of Counterforce: Technological Change and the Future of Nuclear Deterrence', *International Security*, vol. 41, no. 4, Spring 2017, pp. 9–49.

64  Matthew Kroenig, *The Logic of American Nuclear Strategy: Why Strategic Superiority Matters* (New York: Oxford University Press, 2018).

65  James Goldgeier and Lily Wojtowicz, 'Reassurance and Deterrence After Russia's War Against Ukraine', *Security Studies*, vol. 31, no. 4, 2022, pp. 736–43.

66  Reid B.C. Pauly and Rose McDermott, 'The Psychology of Nuclear Brinkmanship', *International Security*, vol. 47, no. 3, 2023, pp. 9–51.

67  Glaser, *Analyzing Strategic Nuclear Policy*, p. 139.

68  Barry R. Posen, *Inadvertent Escalation: Conventional War and Nuclear Risks* (Ithaca, NY: Cornell University Press, 1991).

69  James M. Acton, *Entanglement: How Developments in Nonnuclear Technology*

and *Doctrine Are Raising Unintended Nuclear Escalation Risks and What to Do About Them* (unpublished manuscript, 2024). See also James Johnson, 'Inadvertent Escalation in the Age of Intelligence Machines: A New Model for Nuclear Risk in the Digital Age', *European Journal of International Security*, vol. 7, no. 3, August 2022, pp. 340–1.

70  For an overview of this debate, see Caitlin Talmadge and Joshua Rovner, 'The Meaning of China's Nuclear Modernization', *Journal of Strategic Studies*, vol. 46, nos 6–7, 2023, pp. 1116–48.

71  Fiona S. Cunningham and M. Taylor Fravel, 'Assuring Assured Retaliation: China's Nuclear Posture and US–China Strategic Stability', *International Security*, vol. 40, no. 2, 2015, pp. 7–50; and Hui Zhang, 'China's Nuclear Force Modernization', in Allison Pytlak and Ray Acheson (eds), *Assuring Destruction Forever* (Geneva: Women's International League for Peace and Freedom, 2022), pp. 30–8.

72  A number of defence officials have sounded the alarm about what they fear to be Chinese first-strike capabilities. For examples, see Talmadge and Rovner, 'Meaning of China's Nuclear Revolution', pp. 1127–8. For a pessimistic view of the implications, see Matthew Kroenig and Jeffrey Cimmino, 'Global Strategy 2021: An Allied Strategy for China', Strategy Paper, The Atlantic Council, 16 December 2020, https://www.atlanticcouncil.org/srv/htdocs/wp-content/uploads/2020/12/Global-Strategy-2021%E2%80%94An-Allied-Strategy-for-China-V1-FINAL-1.pdf.

73  Thomas J. Christensen, 'The Meaning of the Nuclear Evolution: China's Strategic Modernization and US–China Security Relations', *Journal of Strategic Studies*, vol. 35, no. 4, 2012, pp. 447–87; and Stacie L. Pettyjohn and Becca Wasser, 'A War in Taiwan Could Go Nuclear', *Foreign Affairs*, 20 May 2022, https://www.foreignaffairs.com/articles/china/2022-05-20/fight-over-taiwan-could-go-nuclear.

## Chapter Four

1  Erik Goepner, 'War State, Trauma State: Why Afghanistan Remains Stuck in Conflict', Cato Institute, Policy Analysis no. 844, 19 June 2018, https://www.cato.org/publications/policy-analysis/war-state-trauma-state-why-afghanistan-remains-stuck-conflict.

2  Thomas Gibbons-Neff, 'A Marine Looks Back on His Battles in Afghanistan', *New York Times*, 16 September 2019.

3  Greg Jaffe, 'Afghanistan Wasn't Destined to Fail. Here's How We Could Have Fought It Better', *Washington Post*, 20 December 2019.

4  Martha Crenshaw, 'Terrorism, Strategies, and Grand Strategies', in Audrey Kurth Cronin and James M. Ludes (eds), *Attacking Terrorism: Elements of a Grand Strategy* (Washington DC: Georgetown University Press, 2004), pp. 74–93.

5  I treat these ideas in more detail in 'The Heroes of COIN', *Orbis*, vol. 56, no. 2, Spring 2012, pp. 215–32; and 'Questions about COIN after Iraq and Afghanistan', in David Martin Jones, Celeste Ward Gventner and M.L.R. Smith (eds), *The New Counterinsurgency Era in Critical Perspective* (London: Palgrave Macmillan, 2014), pp. 299–318. For a recent analysis, see Roger D. Petersen, *Death, Dominance, and State-building: The US in Iraq and the Future of American Military Intervention* (Oxford: Oxford University Press, 2024).

6    Council on Foreign Relations Task Force, 'Improving the US Public Diplomacy Campaign in the War Against Terrorism', November 2001, https://www.cfr.org/report/improving-us-public-diplomacy-campaign-war-against-terrorism.

7    Pew Research Center, 'Anti-Americanism: Causes and Characteristics', 10 December 2003, https://www.pewresearch.org/global/2003/12/10/anti-americanism-causes-and-characteristics/.

8    The Biden administration banned signature strikes in 2022. See Charlie Savage, 'Biden Rules Tighten Limits on Drone Strikes', New York Times, 1 July 2023. For background, see Lynn E. Davis, Michael McNerney and Michael D. Greenberg, 'Clarifying the Rules of Targeted Killing: An Analytical Framework for Policies Involving Long-range Armed Drones', Research Report RR-1610-OSF, RAND Corporation, 2016, https://www.rand.org/pubs/research_reports/RR1610.html.

9    Jacqueline L. Hazelton, 'Drone Strikes and Grand Strategy: Toward a Political Understanding of the Uses of Unmanned Aerial Vehicle Attacks in US Security Policy', Journal of Strategic Studies, vol. 40, nos 1–2, 2016, pp. 68–91, at p. 83; and Audrey Kurth Cronin, 'Why Drones Fail', Foreign Affairs, vol. 92, no. 4, July–August 2013, pp. 44–54.

10   Curtis A. Bradley and Jack S. Goldsmith, 'Obama's AUMF Legacy', American Journal of International Law, vol. 110, no. 4, 2016, pp. 628–45.

11   Linda Robinson, 'Special Ops Global Whack-a-Mole', USA Today, 8 April 2013.

12   Spencer Ackerman, Reign of Terror: How the 9/11 Era Destabilized America and Produced Trump (New York: Viking, 2021).

13   Rosa Brooks offers a half dozen. See 'US Counterterrorism Strategy Is the Definition of Insanity', Foreign Policy,

24 June 2015, https://foreignpolicy.com/2015/06/24/u-s-counterterrorism-strategy-is-the-definition-of-insanity/.

14   Carl von Clausewitz, On War, trans. and ed. Michael Howard and Peter Paret (Princeton, NJ: Princeton University Press, 1976), p. 75.

15   For examples, see Robert F. Trager and Dessislava P. Zagorcheva, 'Deterring Terrorism: It Can Be Done', International Security, vol. 30, no. 3, 2006, pp. 83–123; Matthew Kroenig and Barry Pavel, 'How to Deter Terrorism', Washington Quarterly, vol. 35, no. 2, 2012, pp. 21–36; and Andreas Wenger and Alex Wilner (eds), Deterring Terrorism: Theory and Practice (Stanford, CA: Stanford University Press, 2012).

16   Alex S. Wilner, Deterring Rational Fanatics (Philadelphia, PA: University of Pennsylvania Press, 2015).

17   Daniel Byman, 'Whatever Happened to al Qaeda?', Foreign Policy, 31 January 2023, https://foreignpolicy.com/2023/07/31/al-qaeda-zawahiri-death-strength-decline-terrorism/.

18   Aki Peritz and Eric Rosenbach, Find, Fix, Finish: Inside the Counterterrorism Campaigns that Killed bin Laden and Devastated al Qaeda (New York: Public Affairs, 2012). For a doctrinal description of the targeting process, see Joint Chiefs of Staff, 'Counterterrorism', Joint Publication 3–26, 24 October 2014, pp. V3–V6, https://www.hsdl.org/c/abstract/?docid=759133.

19   The so-called Islamic State is an exception. It attempted to create a territorial state in Iraq and Syria, along with a conventional military force. Doing so gave it an impressive facade but also made it particularly vulnerable to attack. Ido Levy, Soldiers of End-times: Assessing the Military Effectiveness of the Islamic State (Lanham, MD: Rowman & Littlefield, 2023).

20   'Once the expenditure of effort exceeds the value of the political object',

Clausewitz wrote, 'the object must be renounced and peace must follow'. Knowing when to say when is difficult in conventional wars against state enemies, but at least in those cases there are formal mechanisms for peace negotiations. Nothing similar is possible in the United States' war on terrorism, given the amorphous and changing nature of transnational armed groups. Clausewitz, *On War*, p. 92.

21  'Remarks by President Biden on the Drawdown of US Forces in Afghanistan', 8 July 2021, https://www.whitehouse.gov/briefing-room/speeches-remarks/2021/07/08/remarks-by-president-biden-on-the-drawdown-of-u-s-forces-in-afghanistan/.

22  *Ibid*.

23  'Written Testimony of Dr. Colin F. Jackson to the Senate Armed Services Committee', 11 February 2020, https://www.armed-services.senate.gov/imo/media/doc/Jackson_02-11-20.pdf.

24  The notion of an 'end state' is popular among military officers. For a recent example, see Richard E. Berkebile, 'Military Strategy Revisited: A Critique of the Lykke Formulation', *Military Review*, May 2018, https://www.armyupress.army.mil/Portals/7/Army-Press-Online-Journal/documents/Berkebile-v2.pdf.

25  US Department of Defense, 'US Military Casualties – Operation Freedom's Sentinel (OFS) Casualty Summary by Month and Service', Defense Casualties Analysis System, 2024, https://dcas.dmdc.osd.mil/dcas/app/conflictCasualties/ofs/byMonth.

26  US Representative Dan Crenshaw (for Texas's 2nd congressional district) gave a representative argument in an op-ed shortly after the US withdrawal: 'There are a lot of foreign policy options between nation building and giving up. We found the proper balance in recent years – maintaining a small force that propped up the Afghan government while also giving us the capability to strike at Taliban and other terrorist networks as needed.' Dan Crenshaw, 'The "Endless War" Fallacy', *Wall Street Journal*, 17 August 2021.

27  Xenia Wickett, 'Why the United States Remains an Indispensable Nation', Chatham House, 30 June 2015, https://www.chathamhouse.org/expert/comment/why-united-states-remains-indispensable-nation.

28  Recent critiques include Richard K. Betts, 'The Grandiosity of Grand Strategy', *Washington Quarterly*, vol. 42, no. 4, 2019, pp. 7–22; and David M. Edelstein and Ronald R. Krebs, 'Delusions of Grand Strategy', *Foreign Affairs*, vol. 94, no. 6, 2015, pp. 109–16.

29  This discussion draws on Joshua Rovner, 'The War on Terrorism as Imperial Policing', *War on the Rocks*, 2 November 2017, https://warontherocks.com/2017/11/the-war-on-terrorism-as-imperial-policing/.

30  David E. Omissi, *Airpower and Colonial Control: The Royal Air Force, 1919–1939* (Manchester: Manchester University Press, 1990); and Priya Satia, 'The Defense of Inhumanity: Air Control and the British Idea of Arabia', *American Historical Review*, vol. 11, no. 1, 2006, pp. 16–51.

31  Marek Pruszewicz, 'The 1920s British Air Bombing Campaign in Iraq', BBC, 7 October 2014, https://www.bbc.com/news/magazine-29441383.

32  David Killingray, '"A Swift Agent of Government": Air Power in British Colonial Africa, 1916–1939', *Journal of African History*, vol. 25, no. 4, October 1984, pp. 429–44.

33  Secretary of defense Donald Rumsfeld was the face of this approach. His eponymous doctrine emphasised the use of technologically sophisticated special-operations forces, who could work in concert with precision airpower to achieve outsize results. See Donald Rumsfeld, 'Transforming the Military', *Foreign Affairs*, vol. 81, no. 3, 2002, pp. 20–32.

Similar arguments were popular in the 1990s, when the US enjoyed an overwhelming technological advantage. See especially Douglas A. Macgregor, *Breaking the Phalanx: A New Design for Landpower in the 21st Century* (Westport, CT: Praeger, 1997); and William A. Owens and Edward Offley, *Lifting the Fog of War* (New York: Farrar, Straus and Giroux, 2000).

34  The expansion of US aims in Afghanistan, however, required more forces. The shift from a narrow counter-terrorism mission to a much more expansive state-building project implied the need for many more boots on the ground. As a result, US forces not only called on active-duty personnel for repeated deployments, but also increasingly turned to Reserve and National Guard forces. For a discussion of the effects, see Mara Karlin, *The Inheritance: America's Military After Two Decades of War* (Washington DC: Brookings Institution Press, 2021); and Carrie A. Lee, 'A Full Diagnosis of Civil–

Military Health Should Include the National Guard and Reserves', *Texas National Security Review* (forthcoming).

35  Conor Friedersdorf, 'The Obama Administration's Drone-strike Dissembling', *Atlantic*, 14 March 2016, https://www.theatlantic.com/politics/archive/2016/03/the-obama-administrations-drone-strike-dissembling/473541/.

36  Analysts with different grand-strategic preferences agree on this point. Compare Benjamin H. Friedman and Justin Logan, 'Why the US Military Budget Is "Foolish and Sustainable"', *Orbis*, vol. 56, no. 2, Spring 2012, pp. 177–91; and Stephen G. Brooks and William C. Wohlforth, *World Out of Balance: International Relations and the Challenge of American Primacy* (Princeton, NJ: Princeton University Press, 2008).

37  Michael C. Horowitz, 'Do Emerging Military Technologies Matter for International Politics?', *Annual Review of Political Science*, vol. 23, 2020, pp. 385–400.

## Chapter Five

1  Thomas G. Mahnken, *Technology and the American Way of War Since 1945* (New York: Columbia University Press, 2010).
2  Joshua Rovner, 'Warfighting and Cyberspace', in Emily Goldman, Michael Warner and Jacquelyn Schneider (eds), *Ten Years In: Implementing Strategic Approaches to Cyberspace* (Newport, RI: US Naval War College, Newport Papers, 2021), pp. 81–96.
3  US Department of Defense, *Military and Security Developments Involving the People's Republic of China*, 2023, p. 156, https://media.defense.gov/2023/Oct/19/2003323409/-1/-1/1/2023-MILITARY-AND-SECURITY-DEVELOPMENTS-INVOLVING-THE-PEOPLES-REPUBLIC-OF-CHINA.PDF.

4  *Ibid.*
5  Quoted in 'Artificial Intelligence is Changing Every Aspect of War', *The Economist*, 7 September 2019.
6  National Security Commission on Artificial Intelligence, 'Final Report', 2021, p. 7, https://reports.nscai.gov/final-report/.
7  Curtis Peebles, *High Frontier: The U.S. Air Force and the Military Space Program* (Washington DC: Air Force Historical Studies Office, 1997). On the special challenges of operating in space, see Rebecca Reesman and James Wilson, 'Physics Gets a Vote: No Starcruisers for Space Force', *War on the Rocks*, 28 June 2021, https://warontherocks.com/2021/06/physics-gets-a-vote-no-starcruisers-for-space-force/.

8   William A. Owens and Edward Offley, *Lifting the Fog of War* (New York: Farrar, Straus and Giroux, 2000).

9   Bryan R. Early and Erik Gartzke, 'Spying from Space: Reconnaissance Satellites and Interstate Disputes', *Journal of Conflict Resolution*, vol. 65, no. 9, 2021, pp. 1551–75; and Joshua Rovner, 'Spies as Agents of Peace', in Kurt Almqvist, Alastair Benn and Mattias Hessérus (eds), *Man and Technology: How Humanity Thrives in a Changing World* (Stockholm: Bokförlaget Stolpe, 2022), pp. 187–195.

10  Aaron Bateman, 'Trust but Verify: Satellite Reconnaissance, Secrecy and Arms Control During the Cold War', *Journal of Strategic Studies*, vol. 46, no. 5, 2023, pp. 1037–61; and Elena Grossfield, 'Russia's Declining Satellite Reconnaissance Capabilities and Its Implications for Security and International Stability', *International Journal of Intelligence and Counterintelligence* (forthcoming).

11  Some argue that US space policy sought military superiority from its earliest days. For an elaboration of this claim and a useful overview of the evolution of space strategy, see Bleddyn E. Bowen, *Original Sin: Power, Technology, and War in Outer Space* (Oxford: Oxford University Press, 2023).

12  Aaron Bateman, 'Why Russia Might Put a Nuclear Weapon in Space', *Foreign Affairs*, 7 March 2024, https://www.foreignaffairs.com/russian-federation/why-russia-might-put-nuclear-weapon-space. The use of nuclear weapons in space could also potentially generate an electromagnetic pulse, with calamitous effects on the ground, as well as irradiating a significant area of space.

13  People's Liberation Army Academy of Military Science, Military Strategy Studies Department, *Science of Military Strategy* (Beijing: Military Science, December 2013), p. 116. Quoted in John Costello and Peter Mattis, 'Electronic Warfare and the Renaissance of Chinese Information Operations', in Joe McReynolds (ed.), *China's Evolving Military Strategy* (Washington DC: Jamestown Foundation, 2016), p. 165.

14  Jane Zhang and Jesse Levine, 'Why AI Is Next Flashpoint in US–China Tech Rivalry', *Washington Post*, 29 June 2023.

15  Jiang and Hu are quoted in Fiona S. Cunningham, *Under the Nuclear Shadow: China's Information-age Weapons in International Security* (Princeton, NJ: Princeton University Press, 2024). On China's enthusiasm for space under Xi Jinping, see Khyle Eastin, 'A Domain of Great Powers: The Strategic Role of Space in Achieving China's Dream of National Rejuvenation', *National Bureau of Asian Research*, 10 May 2024, https://strategicspace.nbr.org/a-domain-of-great-powers-the-strategic-role-of-space-in-achieving-chinas-dream-of-national-rejuvenation/.

16  For a longer treatment of this question, see Joshua Rovner, 'Strategy and Grand Strategy in New Domains', in Hal Brands (ed.), *The New Makers of Modern Strategy: From the Ancient World to the Digital Age* (Princeton, NJ: Princeton University Press, 2023), pp. 1067–91.

17  Both sides did invest in counter-space electronic warfare, however, which extended technologies used in other domains. I thank Aaron Bateman for pointing this out. On the long-standing debate over the definition of 'space weapons', see Svetla Ben-Itzhak, *Space Security* (unpublished manuscript, currently under review).

18  Jordan Branch, 'What's in a Name? Metaphors and Cybersecurity', *International Organization*, vol. 75, no. 1, Winter 2021, pp. 39–70; Erick

D. McCroskey and Charles A.
Mock, 'Operational Graphics for
Cyberspace', *Joint Force Quarterly*, no.
85, 2017, pp. 42–9; and Ian Reynolds,
'AI Enabled Command in the United
States: Rhetorical Contestation and
Solving the Problems of Speed and
Knowledge in War', PhD dissertation,
American University, 2024.

19  John Arquilla and David Ronfeldt,
'Cyberwar Is Coming!', in Arquilla
and Ronfeldt (eds), *In Athena's Camp:
Preparing for the Next Conflict in the
Information Age* (Santa Monica, CA:
RAND, 1997 [1993]).

20  Thomas Rid, 'Cyberwar Will Not
Take Place', *Journal of Strategic Studies*,
vol. 35, no. 1, 2012, pp. 5–32.

21  Rovner, 'Warfighting in Cyberspace'.
For a Cold War analogy, see Jonathan
Reed Winkler, 'The Forgotten Menace
of Electro-magnetic Warfare in the
Early Cold War', *Diplomatic History*,
vol. 42, no. 2, 2018, pp. 254–80.

22  Jacqueline Schneider, *Digitally Enabled
Warfare: The Capability–Vulnerability
Paradox* (Washington DC: Center for a
New American Security, 2016).

23  Joshua Rovner, 'Everything,
Everywhere, All at Once?
Cyberspace Operations and Chinese
Strategy', *War on the Rocks*, 25
March 2024, https://warontherocks.
com/2024/03/everything-
everywhere-all-at-once-cyberspace-
operations-and-chinese-strategy/. On
the limits of information campaigns,
see Gavin Wilde, 'From Panic
to Policy: The Limits of Foreign
Propaganda and the Foundations of
an Effective Response', *Texas National
Security Review*, vol. 7, no. 2, 2024,
pp. 42–55.

24  Max Smeets, *No Shortcuts: Why States
Struggle to Develop a Military Cyber-
force* (Oxford: Oxford University
Press, 2022).

25  On the organisational history of
US Cyber Command, see Michael
Warner, 'US Cyber Command's First

Decade', Hoover Institution, Aegis
Series Paper no. 2008, 2020, https://
www.hoover.org/sites/default/files/
research/docs/warner_webready.
pdf. On the professionalisation of
military cyberspace, see Rebecca
Slayton, '(De)Stabilizing Cyber
Warriors: The Emergence of US
Military Cyber Expertise, 1967–2018',
in Robert Chesney, James Shires and
Max Smeets (eds), *Cyberspace and
Instability* (Edinburgh: Edinburgh
University Press, 2023), pp. 177–214.
For a recent argument in favor of a
cyber force, see Erica Lonergan and
Mark Montgomery, 'United States
Cyber Force: A Defense Imperative',
Foundation for the Defense of
Democracies, 25 March 2024, https://
www.fdd.org/analysis/2024/03/25/
united-states-cyber-force/.

26  Nina Kollars and Emma Moore,
'Every Marine a Blue-haired Quasi-
rifleperson?', *War on The Rocks*, 21
August 2019, https://warontherocks.
com/2019/08/every-marine-a-blue-
haired-quasi-rifleperson/.

27  Georgia Tech's School of Public Policy
provides a useful online primer for
internet-governance debates: https://
www.internetgovernance.org/
what-is-internet-governance/.

28  Laura DeNardis, *The Internet in
Everything: Freedom and Security in a
World with No Off Switch* (New Haven,
CT: Yale University Press, 2020).

29  Jon R. Lindsay, *Information Technology
and Military Power* (Ithaca, NY:
Cornell University Press, 2020).

30  Max Smeets, 'A Matter of Time: On the
Transitory Nature of Cyberweapons',
*Journal of Strategic Studies*, vol. 41, nos
1–2, 2018, pp. 6–32.

31  For discussions of the trade-offs and
technical limitations of cyberspace
operations, see Erica D. Lonergan
and Shawn W. Lonergan, *Escalation
Dynamics in Cyberspace* (Oxford: Oxford
University Press, 2023); and Lennart
Maschmeyer, *Subversion: From Covert*

*Action to Cyber Conflict* (Oxford: Oxford University Press, 2024).

32  Chris Dougherty, 'Confronting Chaos: A New Concept for Information Advantage', *War on the Rocks*, 9 September 2021, https://warontherocks.com/2021/09/confronting-chaos-a-new-concept-for-information-advantage/.

33  Recent commentary includes Hal Brands, 'Win or Lose, US War Against China or Russia Won't Be Short', *Bloomberg*, 14 June 2021; Andrew F. Krepenevich, Jr, *Protracted Great Power War: A Preliminary Assessment* (Washington DC: Center for a New American Security, 2020); Iskander Rehman, *Planning for Protraction: A Historically Informed Approach to Great-power War and Sino-US Competition* (Abingdon: Routledge for the IISS, 2024); and Joshua Rovner, 'Two Kinds of Catastrophe: Nuclear Escalation and Protracted War in Asia', *Journal of Strategic Studies*, vol. 40, no. 5, 2017, pp. 696–730.

34  Nineteenth-century undersea telegraph-cable networks are similar in that they both facilitated Britain's maritime trading empire and also helped coordinate its global military activities. Leaders speculated that cable-cutting would be common in future wars; those fears have recently re-emerged. See Daniel R. Headrick, *The Invisible Weapon: Telecommunications and International Politics, 1851–1945* (Oxford: Oxford University Press, 1991); and Aaron Bateman, 'Undersea Cables and the Vulnerability of American Power', *Englesberg Ideas*, 7 May 2024, https://engelsbergideas.com/essays/undersea-cables-and-the-vulnerability-of-american-power/.

35  Joshua Rovner and Tyler Moore, 'Does the Internet Need a Hegemon?', *Journal of Global Security Studies*, vol. 2, no. 3, 2017, pp. 184–203.

36  The former commander of US Cyber Command argued that 'peer and near-peer competitors operate continuously against us in cyberspace. These activities are not isolated hacks or incidents, but strategic campaigns. Cyberspace provides our adversaries with new ways to mount continuous, nonviolent operations that produce cumulative, strategic impacts by eroding US military, economic, and political power without reaching a threshold that triggers an armed response.' Paul M. Nakasone, 'A Cyber Force for Persistent Operations', *Joint Force Quarterly*, vol. 92, 2019, pp. 10–14, at p. 11. For the theory underlying these warnings, see Michael P. Fischerkeller, Emily O. Goldman and Richard J. Harknett, *Cyber Persistence Theory: Redefining National Security in Cyberspace* (Oxford: Oxford University Press, 2022).

37  Paul M. Nakasone and Michael Sulmeyer, 'How to Compete in Cyberspace', *Foreign Affairs*, 25 August 2020, https://www.foreignaffairs.com/articles/united-states/2020-08-25/cybersecurity. See also Fisherkeller, Goldman and Harknett, *Cyber Persistence Theory*.

38  Tom Johansmeyer, 'Why Natural Catastrophes Will Always Be Worse than Cyber Catastrophes', *War on the Rocks*, 5 April 2024, https://warontherocks.com/2024/04/why-natural-catastrophes-will-always-be-worse-than-cyber-catastrophes/.

39  Patrick Tucker, 'Chinese Hacking Operations Have Entered a Far More Dangerous Phase, US Warns', *Defense One*, 1 February 2024, https://www.defenseone.com/technology/2024/02/chinese-hacking-operations-have-entered-far-more-dangerous-phase-us-warns/393843/.

40  This section draws on Joshua Rovner, 'Sabotage and War in Cyberspace', *War on the Rocks*, 19 July 2022.

41  David Sanger, *The Perfect Weapon: War, Sabotage, and Fear in the Cyber Age* (New York: Crown, 2018).

42  Nicole Perlroth, *This Is How They Tell Me the World Ends: The Cyberweapons Arms Race* (London: Bloomsbury, 2021).

43  On the practical challenges of conducting offensive cyberspace operations, see Jon R. Lindsay, 'Stuxnet and the Limits of Cyber Warfare', *Security Studies*, vol. 22, no. 3, 2013, pp. 365–404; Thomas Rid and Peter McBurney, 'Cyber-Weapons', *RUSI Journal*, vol. 157, no. 1, 2012, pp. 6–13; and Rovner, 'Warfighting in Cyberspace'.

44  Microsoft Digital Security Unit, 'An Overview of Russia's Cyberattack Activity in Ukraine', 27 April 2022, https://query.prod.cms.rt.microsoft.com/cms/api/am/binary/RE4Vwwd; and Microsoft, 'Defending Ukraine: Early Lessons from the Cyber War', 22 June 2022, https://query.prod.cms.rt.microsoft.com/cms/api/am/binary/RE50KOK.

45  Examples include Nadiya Kostyuk and Eric Gartzke, 'Why Cyber Dogs Have Yet to Bark Loudly in Russia's War in Ukraine', *Texas National Security Review*, vol. 5, no. 3, 2022, pp. 113–26; Stephanie Carvin, 'Is Ukraine the Cyberwar that Wasn't?', *Newsweek*, 22 September 2022; Marcus Willett, 'The Cyber Dimension of the Russia–Ukraine War', *Survival*, vol. 64, no. 5, 2022, pp. 7–26; Gavin Wilde, 'Cyber Operations in Ukraine: Russia's Unmet Expectations', Carnegie Endowment for International Peace, 12 December 2022; Grace B. Mueller et al., 'Cyber Operations During the Russo-Ukrainian War: From Strange Patterns to Alternative Futures', Center for Strategic and International Studies, 13 July 2023; Matthias Schulze and Mika Kerttunen, 'Cyber Operations in Russia's War Against Ukraine: Uses, Limitations, and Lessons Learned So Far', Stiftung Wissenschaft und Politik, 17 April 2023; and Alison Pytlak, 'False Alarms: Reflecting on the Role of Cyber Operations in the Russia–Ukraine War', Stimson Center, 22 February 2024.

46  Christopher Miller and Stephen Bernard, 'Military Briefing: Ukraine Digs Deep as Russia Advances', *Financial Times*, 28 March 2024.

47  Nick Beecroft, 'Evaluating the International Support to Ukrainian Cyber Defense', Carnegie Endowment for International Peace, 3 November 2022; and Mehul Srivastava, 'Ukraine Innovates on Cyber Defense', *Financial Times*, 18 July 2023.

48  Keir Giles, 'Russian Cyber and Information War in Practice', Chatham House, 14 December 2023.

49  Willett, 'The Cyber Dimension of the Russia–Ukraine War'.

50  Maegan Vazquez et al., 'Biden Warns Business Leaders to Prepare for Russian Cyber Attacks', CNN, 22 March 2022.

51  'How Cybercriminals Have Been Affected by the War in Ukraine', *The Economist*, 30 November 2022.

52  Max Smeets and Robert Chesney (eds), *Deter, Disrupt, or Deceive: Assessing Cyber Conflict as an Intelligence Contest* (Washington DC: Georgetown University Press, 2023).

53  This section draws on Rovner, 'Everything, Everywhere, All at Once?'.

54  Office of the Director of National Intelligence, 'Annual Threat Assessment of the US Intelligence Community', 5 February 2024, https://www.dni.gov/files/ODNI/documents/assessments/ATA-2024-Unclassified-Report.pdf.

55  For various accounts of Chinese motives, see William C. Hannas, James Mulvenon and Anna B. Puglisi, *Chinese Industrial Espionage:*

*Technology Acquisition and Military Modernization* (London: Routledge, 2013), pp. 216–29; Mark A. Stokes, 'The Chinese People's Liberation Army Computer Network Operations Infrastructure', in Jon R. Lindsay, Tai Ming Cheung and Derek S. Reveron (eds), *China and Cybersecurity: Espionage, Strategy, and Politics in the Digital Domain* (Oxford: Oxford University Press, 2015), pp. 163–87; Benjamin Jensen, 'How the Chinese Communist Party Uses Cyber Espionage to Undermine the American Economy', Statement before the House Judiciary Subcommittee on Courts, Intellectual Property and the Internet, 19 October 2023; and 'What to Make of China's Massive Cyber Espionage Campaign', *The Economist*, 26 March 2024.

56 James A. Siebens and Melanie Sisson, 'China's Multi-domain Deterrence of the United States', in James A. Siebens (ed.), *China's Use of Armed Coercion: To Win Without Fighting* (London: Routledge, 2024), pp. 202–16.

57 Chinese nuclear modernisation might also contribute to this strategy. Superior regional nuclear forces might serve to keep a China–Taiwan conflict 'bilateral'. Rather than threatening nuclear strikes against the US itself, theatre nuclear forces might deter US entry in a regional war. See Evan Braden Montgomery and Toshi Yoshihara, 'The Real Challenge of China's Nuclear Modernization', *Washington Quarterly*, vol. 45, no. 4, 2022, pp. 45–60.

58 Quoted in Rovner, 'Everything, Everywhere, All at Once?'.

59 Phil Haun (ed.), *Lectures of the Air Corps Tactical School and American Strategic Bombing in World War II* (Lexington: University of Kentucky Press, 2019).

60 Recent analyses highlighting the economic damage inflicted by airpower include Adam Tooze, *The Wages of Destruction: The Making and Breaking of the Nazi Economy* (New York: Penguin, 2006); and Philips Payson O'Brien, *How the War Was Won: Air–Sea Power and Allied Victory in World War II* (Cambridge: Cambridge University Press, 2015).

61 For a recent example, see Laila Kearney, 'US Electric Grid Growing More Vulnerable to Cyberattacks, Regulator Says', Reuters, 4 April 2024.

62 By contrast, it is not difficult to model the effects of a 2,000-pound bomb on different structures.

63 On the challenges of public–private partnerships in cyberspace, see Madeline Carr, 'Public–Private Partnerships in National Cyber-security Strategies', *International Affairs*, vol. 92, no. 1, 2016, pp. 43–62.

64 Sarah Kreps and Jacquelyn Schneider, 'Escalation Firebreaks in the Cyber, Conventional, and Nuclear Domains: Moving Beyond Effects-based Logics', *Journal of Cybersecurity*, vol. 5, no. 1, 2019, pp. 1–11; and Lonergan and Lonergan, *Escalation Dynamics in Cyberspace*.

65 Compare Patrick Porter, *The False Promise of Liberal Order: Nostalgia, Delusion, and the Rise of Trump* (Cambridge: Polity, 2020); and Michael Poznansky, *In the Shadow of International Law: Secrecy and Regime Change in the Postwar World* (Oxford: Oxford University Press, 2020).

66 Joshua Rovner and Caitlin Talmadge, 'Hegemony, Force Posture, and the Provision of Public Goods: The Once and Future Role of Outside Powers in Securing Persian Gulf Oil', *Security Studies*, vol. 23, no. 3, 2014, pp. 548–81.

67 Joshua Rovner, 'Theory of Sabotage', *Etudes Françaises de Renseignement et de Cyber*, vol. 1, no. 1, 2023, pp. 139–53.

## Conclusion

1 'France Estimates that 150,000 Russian Soldiers Have Been Killed in the Ukraine War', France24.com, 3 May 2024, https://www.france24.com/en/europe/20240503-france-estimates-that-150-000-russian-soldiers-have-been-killed-in-the-ukraine-war.

2 Efraim Inbar and Eitan Shamir, '"Mowing the Grass": Israel's Strategy for Protracted Intractable Conflict', *Journal of Strategic Studies*, vol. 37, no. 1, 2014, pp. 65–90.

3 Helene Cooper et al., 'In Gaza, Israel's Military Has Reached the End of the Line, US Officials Say', *New York Times*, 14 August 2024; and Daniel Estrin, 'Israel Has No Plan for Gaza After Hamas Rule, the Israeli Defense Chief Says', National Public Radio, 16 May 2024, https://www.npr.org/2024/05/16/1251564884/israel-gaza-day-after-gallant-netanyahu.

4 J. William Fulbright, Speech on the Floor of the US Senate, 'The War in Vietnam', 15 June 1965, https://digitalcollections.uark.edu/digital/collection/Fulbright/id/749.

# INDEX

# THE ADELPHI SERIES

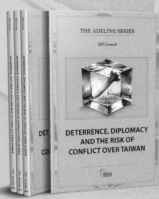

Aaron Connelly &
Shona Loong

## NEW ANSWERS
## TO OLD QUESTIONS

*Myanmar Before and After the 2021 Coup d'État*

**Adelphi 505–507**
published June 2024;
234x156; 184pp;
Paperback: 978-1-032-88380-9
eBook: 978-1-003-53746-5

available at
## amazon

OR

R Routledge
Taylor & Francis Group

**Adelphi 508–510**
published July 2024;
234x156; 188pp;
Paperback: 978-1-032-89633-5
eBook: 978-1-003-54382-4

Bill Emmott

## DETERRENCE,
## DIPLOMACY AND THE
## RISK OF CONFLICT
## OVER TAIWAN

IISS
THE INTERNATIONAL INSTITUTE
FOR STRATEGIC STUDIES

www.iiss.org/publications/adelphi

# THE ADELPHI SERIES

# CYBER OPERATIONS AND THEIR RESPONSIBLE USE

'*Cyber Operations and Their Responsible Use* is a must-read primer for cyber operators, policymakers and national-security professionals. Marcus Willett's work – particularly his thorough coverage of threats and balanced discussion on cyber deterrence – provides new insights and informed analysis that only someone with his impressive background and experience could produce. His writing style draws the reader close to his arguments and provides a clarity not seen before given the complexity of the subject matter.'

**GENERAL PAUL M. NAKASONE**, US Army (Retired), Former Commander, US Cyber Command and Director, National Security Agency

*Marcus Willett*

**IISS**

THE INTERNATIONAL INSTITUTE
FOR STRATEGIC STUDIES

**available at**
**amazon**

**OR**

**Routledge**
Taylor & Francis Group

**Adelphi 511–513**;
published November 2024;
234x156; 360pp;
Paperback: 978-1-032-98909-9
eBook: 978-1-003-60133-3

In the twenty-first century, cyberspace and the 'real world' have become inseparable. The stability and security of cyberspace therefore affect, in increasingly profound ways, the economies, international reputations, national security, military capabilities and global influence of states. In their short history, operations in cyberspace have already been used extensively by states and their non-state supporters for many purposes. They are an inevitable aspect of contemporary international affairs while carrying significant risk.

In this *Adelphi* book, Marcus Willett, a former deputy head of GCHQ, argues that there is no coherent or widely shared understanding of what cyber operations really are, how they are used and what they can do; or of their implications for strategic affairs and international law; or what their 'responsible' use really entails. The myths and misunderstandings that abound tend to dull the conceptual clarity needed by strategic policymakers and overseers, and they complicate the essential task in a liberal democracy of maintaining public consent for, and legitimisation of, the development and use of such capabilities. The book sheds light on these issues, exposing myths and clarifying misunderstandings.

www.iiss.org/publications/adelphi

# JOURNAL SUBSCRIPTION INFORMATION

Six issues per year of the *Adelphi* Series (Print ISSN 1944-5571, Online ISSN 1944-558X) are published by Taylor & Francis Group, 4 Park Square, Milton Park, Abingdon, Oxon, OX14 4RN, UK.

Send address changes to Taylor & Francis Customer Services, Informa UK Ltd., Sheepen Place, Colchester, Essex CO3 3LP, UK.

Subscription records are maintained at Taylor & Francis Group, 4 Park Square, Milton Park, Abingdon, OX14 4RN, UK.

**Subscription information:**
For more information and subscription rates, please see tandfonline.com/pricing/journal/ tadl). Taylor & Francis journals are available in a range of different packages, designed to suit every library's needs and budget. This journal is available for institutional subscriptions with online only or print & online options. This journal may also be available as part of our libraries, subject collections, or archives. For more information on our sales packages, please visit: librarianresources. taylorandfrancis.com.

For support with any institutional subscription, please visit help.tandfonline.com or email our dedicated team at subscriptions@tandf.co.uk.

Subscriptions purchased at the personal rate are strictly for personal, non-commercial use only. The reselling of personal subscriptions is prohibited. Personal subscriptions must be purchased with a personal check, credit card, or BAC/wire transfer. Proof of personal status may be requested.

**Back issues:**
Please visit https://taylorandfrancis.com/ journals/customer-services/ for more information on how to purchase back issues.

**Ordering information:**
To subscribe to the Journal, please contact: T&F Customer Services, Informa UK Ltd, Sheepen Place, Colchester, Essex, CO3 3LP, United Kingdom. Tel: +44 (0) 20 8052 2030; email: subscriptions@tandf.co.uk.

Taylor & Francis journals are priced in USD, GBP and EUR (as well as AUD and CAD for a limited number of journals). All subscriptions are charged depending on where the end customer is based. If you are unsure which rate applies to you, please contact Customer Services. All subscriptions are payable in advance and all rates include postage. We are required to charge applicable VAT/GST on all print and online combination subscriptions, in addition to our online only journals. Subscriptions are entered on an annual basis, i.e., January to December. Payment may be made by sterling check, dollar check, euro check, international money order, National Giro or credit cards (Amex, Visa and Mastercard).

**Disclaimer:** The International Institute for Strategic Studies and our publisher Taylor & Francis make every effort to ensure the accuracy of all the information (the "Content") contained in our publications. However, The International Institute for Strategic Studies and our publisher Taylor & Francis, our agents (including the editor, any member of the editorial team or editorial board, and any guest editors), and our licensors make no representations or warranties whatsoever as to the accuracy, completeness, or suitability for any purpose of the Content. Any opinions and views expressed in this publication are the opinions and views of the authors, and are not the views of or endorsed by The International Institute for Strategic Studies and our publisher Taylor & Francis. The accuracy of the Content should not be relied upon and should be independently verified with primary sources of information. The International Institute for Strategic Studies and our publisher Taylor & Francis shall not be liable for any losses, actions, claims, proceedings, demands, costs, expenses, damages, and other liabilities whatsoever or howsoever caused arising directly or indirectly in connection with, in relation to, or arising out of the use of the Content. Terms & Conditions of access and use can be found at http://www.tandfonline.com/page/terms-and-conditions.

All Taylor & Francis Group journals are printed on paper from renewable sources by accredited partners.